# LIFE IS LIKE A
## Golf Course

# C.D. WOOD

iUniverse, Inc.
Bloomington

# Life is Like a Golfcourse

*Scripture quotations marked (AMP) are taken from the Amplified Bible, Copyright © 1954, 1958, 1962, 1964, 1965, 1987 by The Lockman Foundation. Used by permis-sion. Scripture quotations marked (NASB) are taken from the NEW AMERICAN STAN-DARD BIBLE®, Copyright © 1960, 1962, 1963, 1968, 1971, 1972, 1973, 1975, 1977, 1995 by The Lockman Foundation. Used by permission. Scripture quotations marked (NIV) taken from the HOLY BIBLE, NEW INTERNATIONAL VERSION®. Copy-right © 1973, 1978, 1984 Biblica. Used by permission of Zondervan. All rights reserved. Unless otherwise indicated, all Scripture quotations are taken from the Holy Bi-ble, New Living Translation, copyright © 1996. Used by permission of Tyn-dale House Publishers, Inc., Wheaton, Illinois 60189. All rights reserved. Scripture quotations marked (NCV) taken from the New Century Version. Copyright © 2005 by Thomas Nelson, Inc. Used by permission. All rights reserved.*

*iUniverse books may be ordered through booksellers or by contacting:*

*iUniverse*
*1663 Liberty Drive*
*Bloomington, IN 47403*
*www.iuniverse.com*
*1-800-Authors (1-800-288-4677)*

*ISBN: 978-1-4759-3660-5 (sc)*
*ISBN: 978-1-4759-3661-2 (ebk)*

*Library of Congress Control Number: 2012912265*

*Printed in the United States of America*

*iUniverse rev. date: 07/05/2012*

# DEDICATION

To all golfers and non-golfers alike: Look to Him Who has all the answers you need - for this life and beyond. God really does want to have two-way communication with you.

Ask Him to give you 'ears to hear'. You may be surprised what you hear. Feel free to talk to Him about anything—that's what He's there for.

I can tell you, first-and-foremost—God wants you to know that He loves you unconditionally.

There is nothing you can do, or ever have done, that will ever change that truth.

God loves you! Someone once said, 'God not only loves you, He really likes you!' It's surprising how many people struggle with that simple, yet profound concept. It can be very liberating if we can truly take it to heart.

I encourage you to read on with a heart that is willing to listen to whatever else He is saying to you.

# CONTENTS

# Contents

# AUTHOR'S NOTE

Just a brief note to those who may question my credentials in regards to this book and the subject matter. Personally, I have little regard for titles, and I truly believe that God has no great interest in how many letters are behind someone's name. When Dr. John Smith MD, PHD, DD, or whatever his credentials may be, stands at the gates of heaven, the angels won't be addressing him by his earthly titles. More likely it will be something like,

'Hello Johnny. Let's look and see if your name is in this book.' (The Book of Life) It won't matter how educated he is if his name isn't there.

There's an obscure little story in the Old Testament of a poor wise man . (Ecclesiastes 9:14,15) When an enemy army came to attack the city that he lived in, it was through the wise counsel of this uneducated poor man that the city was saved from destruction.

I have been a Christian since November 1980. Over the years I have attended many seminars and studied numerous teachings of a wide variety of biblical and spiritual subjects. The accumulated knowledge gained would've translated into a doctorate years ago, if the courses had been formally accredited. But what if they were accredited? What if I had a string of letters following my name? They only serve to impress those who look for that kind of pedigree so as to provide a reason to accept or reject what the author has to say.

If I were to put any letters after my name, perhaps it would read as follows; C.D.Wood, BA,BSFB - Born Again, Baptized, Spirit Filled Believer!

The name of satan is not capitalized in this book. I choose not to acknowledge him, even to the point of violating grammatical rules.

# INTRODUCTION

*"Set your mind on the things above, not on the things that are on earth."* (Colossians 3:2, NASB)

Do you like to golf? Ever thought much about heaven?

When I was thirteen years old, my dad bought a membership for me at a nearby Golf Club. I'd often walk over, wheeling my clubs behind me on a homemade cart, and play a round or two. I was never too concerned about how well I scored, which was probably why I was able to enjoy myself so much.

This particular Club was especially beautiful, with lots of mature trees and interesting fairways sculpted over low, rolling hills. My favourite time of day to play was early evening, as shadows stretched across the greens and the air was clearer than during the heat of mid-afternoon. I'd take it all in with a quiet sense of exhilaration. At times like these, I could imagine heaven being like a golf course—everything seemed perfect.

Usually, it can be difficult to try to visualize what something in the spiritual realm might be like. It's even harder to put spiritual concepts into words. Jesus knew our limited capacity for understanding things of the Spirit. That's why He often spoke to people using stories or parables. Whoever He was with, He always used images they could relate to, whether it was farmers, shepherds, fishermen or even the religious leaders.

Jesus is still speaking to the hearts of people today in the same personal way. He is just as concerned with relating to people in a way in which they can understand.

In fact, *there is urgency like never before,* in heaven and on earth, to reveal to men and women *truths* about the Kingdom of Heaven—of God's love towards man—but also of His impending judgment and wrath, soon to be released upon the nations of this rebellious world. The peoples of this beleaguered world need to hear the Good News of salvation through Jesus Christ, His only begotten Son, who paid the price for all our sins with His own Blood!

So, what does all this have to do with golf courses? Please allow me to explain.

A few years ago, I worked on a golf course as it was being built. It was during these months—as I watched it evolve from rough, rutted hills to lush, green fairways—that the Holy Spirit began to teach me some insightful truths and comparisons to life. I've attempted to clarify these thoughts with scripture and put them on paper to share with you.

I was reminded that in the mayhem of everyday living, we soon forget about the greater realities of the spiritual realm, and are not alert to what the Spirit of God is doing or saying in the world today. This little book is simply a *vehicle* to direct heart and mind from *earthly things* onto *things above.*

My prayer is that Father in heaven will, by His Spirit, reveal Jesus to whomever reads this and that the following pages may offer encouragement to those who may be struggling in their walk with the Lord, or who may not yet have been *reconciled* with God and are seeking some answers or direction.

I've referred to God's Word quite strongly throughout each chapter, for very good reason—it is our guide, our map to follow throughout life.

Second Timothy 3:16–17 says:

*Every Scripture is God-breathed (given by His inspiration) and profitable for instruction, for reproof and conviction of sin, for correction of error and discipline in obedience, [and] for training in righteousness (in holy living, in conformity to God's will in thought, purpose, and action), so that the man of God may be complete and proficient, well fitted and thoroughly equipped for every good work. (AMP)*

I don't think I've ever been on a golf course which didn't have a map on the back of the scorecard and/or sign-posts along the way to guide you. Even with these, there have been some very confusing times as I've tried to figure out where the next hole is supposed to be. It's always so much easier if I have someone with me who's familiar with the layout.

It isn't God's idea that we should stumble through life going down the wrong fairway. He has provided the map, complete with signposts, *and* He has promised to walk with us every step to keep us from getting lost!

As you begin to read the following pages, won't you start first by asking Him to show you His truth? Are you willing to open your heart and trust Him enough to come in and begin to teach you how to reduce some of the needless strokes we all rack up? He will rescue you from whatever *rough* you may be bogged down in, and will give you a free lift back into the centre of the fairway!

Ask Jesus to be your partner today! Don't take a rain cheque!

> *Behold, now is the acceptable time, now is the day of salvation. (2 Corinthians 6:2, NASB)*

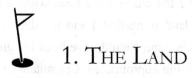

# 1. The Land

## (Counting the Cost)

> *But don't begin until you count the cost. For who would begin construction of a building without first getting estimates and then checking to see if there is enough money to pay the bills? Otherwise, you might complete only the foundation before running out of funds. And then how everyone would laugh at you! They would say, "There's the person who started that building and ran out of money before it was finished!" (Luke 14:28–30, NLT)*

THERE IS AN AMAZING SIMILARITY between the making of a golf course and the construction of a Christian. Two words that apply to both would be *time* and *commitment*.

Before starting a golf course, a great deal of consideration must be given to the costs involved and what kind of commitment is truly required. This, of course, goes without saying to someone with any sense of business responsibility. Once the basics have been worked through (e.g., how much land is needed?) and the decision to proceed is reached, the land should have been bought or be in the process of being appropriated. Consultants, architects, and contractors are now brought into the picture and questions are brought before these experienced professionals in an effort to define the objective. All costs are carefully planned out step by step and arrangements are made to ensure continuous cash flow.

In the world of business, when there's a lot of money involved, decisions tend to be very careful and deliberate.

Someone who wants to become a Christian needs no less amount of time, considering the commitment they are about to make. How much of their lives are they willing to allow God to be God of? They must realize that it's an all-or-nothing decision!

People in North America, Britain and most of Europe don't face the same challenges as many in other countries where Christianity isn't the main demographic. In many places of the world—such as North Korea, China, certain parts of India and the Middle East—the choice to become a believer and follower of Jesus Christ carries with it great risk. Even today, people are beaten, tortured, persecuted, and killed simply for choosing to be identified as *Christian*.

Fortunately, God has His agents on the job, helping those who are at risk to have the courage to make right choices.

*Are not all angels ministering spirits sent to serve those who will inherit salvation? (Hebrews 1:14, NIV)*

I was raised in the church. There have been times in my life when, in retrospect, I know that God was very much involved. I was baptized as a baby in the Presbyterian Church, and as I grew up my family joined the United Church, where I went to Sunday school. When I became a teenager, we moved and attended a Presbyterian church again. I was given the choice to attend or not. Usually, I chose not to. However, as I approached my sixteenth birthday, I remember being interested in checking out the youth group that met at our church, which was just down the street from our house.

Before I could do that, I had a conversation with someone who I really looked up to. They were agnostic and challenged my interest in God with the usual arguments, such as, if God really exists, how could He allow such terrible things to happen in the world? Now remember, at this point in life, all I knew was basic religion, based on a sense of duty to attend. Because of this new influence, I made a complete turnaround in my beliefs. Within the space of a couple of weeks, I went from feeling drawn to join with other young people at the nearby youth group to being totally convinced that God was just a figment of people's imaginations. Remember that quote from scripture about angels being sent as ministering spirits to help guide us? I believe that they were, indeed, present back then, but someone playing the devil's advocate swayed me the wrong direction.

That's not unlike the business world, where unscrupulous agents will try to influence and draw clients from rival companies.

It was, however, clearly *my decision* to reject God. It was a path I followed for several years. As I approached my twenty-fourth birthday, there were numerous incidents when my belief system was challenged. I began to be aware that there was a realm outside the normal physical world, and was fascinated by stories of the paranormal. I was also enrolled in art college at this time, and my involvement with hallucinogenic drugs certainly helped to alter my worldview.

As I said earlier, in retrospect, I can see how God used the circumstances of my life to begin to change my agnostic ideology. In my last year of college, I discovered a program on television (*The 700 Club*), where people talked about miraculous things that God had supposedly done in their lives. Their stories piqued my curiosity and I tuned in regularly. I also began to realize my need for moral stability. My lifestyle and personal choices over the past few years had steadily declined, but with this awakening—or should I say, this reawakened awareness of God—I began to understand that I needed help.

Now, at the same time that the Spirit of God was drawing me, dark *agents* were very active in trying to take me in the opposite direction. I was befriended by a fellow who lived in the same apartment building as I did. As I said before, I was in my last year of college, and I was living with my dad. Dad was often away for days at a time, so when I wasn't in school I was invited to my new friend's apartment for supper. Good food, alcohol and some free *smoke* was very appealing. Eventually I learned that this fellow was a bisexual prostitute and he thought that I should try his way of living, too. He put forth a rather convincing argument as far as the money was concerned, but I certainly *wasn't* interested—at all. Over the months, though, as I got to know him better, the offer was continuously there.

All this time, I still watched *The 700 Club* regularly. I also found a bible, which my dad had buried in a drawer, and began reading it.

Can you see the dynamic that was going on around me? On the one hand, I was being drawn towards the *light*, and on the other, *darkness*.

God will not violate or override our free will, but He is standing by, always ready to respond to our cry for help, however faint it may be.

> *God looks down from heaven on the entire hu-*
> *man race; he looks to see if there is even one*

*with real understanding, one who seeks for God.*
*(Psalm 53:2, NLT)*

*Then you will call upon Me and come and pray to*
*Me and I will listen to you. And you will seek Me*
*and find Me when you search for Me with all your*
*heart. "And I will be found by you," declares the*
*Lord... (Jeremiah 29:12–14, NASB)*

Fortunately, God heard me the night when I had made up my mind to *give in* to the temptation and see if my friend's lifestyle would work for me. Since I was finished with college and needed money, the financial gain was a very practical and appealing benefit. I remember leaning against the countertop in his kitchen, barely able to stand because I had finished his bottle of whiskey. After *considerable* deliberation over the past few weeks, I had made up my mind to go through with this change in direction for my life, but I certainly couldn't do it sober! I remember, as I pushed myself away from the counter and stepped towards the doorway into the living room, I lifted a quick prayer to God. It was to the effect, "God, if you're real, you had better do something, because I've made up my mind to go ahead with this."

Well, as soon as I stepped through from the kitchen to the living room, *I was sober*. I mean—instantly—stone-cold sober! I was shocked. I knew that God had answered my prayer, but that stubborn part of me rose up and became quite perturbed, to say the least. It had taken a long time for me to come to the decision to do this and I was determined to go ahead with it. I asked for some marijuana and we smoked it together—but that had *no effect* on me either.

When I finally went home later on, I realized how God really had heard my heart and prevented something terrible from happening. In that moment of realization, I broke down and told God I was sorry. This was the first time in almost ten years that I had actually wept. It only lasted about a minute, but the relief and peace that flooded in was amazing.

Shortly after this incident, I had to vacate the apartment and ended up in another city, living with my oldest brother. It was only a couple of months after the move that I prayed with the co-host of *The 700 Club* to accept Jesus Christ as my Lord and Saviour.

That's a brief version of how I chose to be reconciled with God. To keep with the theme of this book, I decided that I would accept His offer of a *free lift* from the mess my life was becoming.

*This is a decision that we all have to make.*

We all have to come to terms with questions like why do we need God? What is the Day of Judgment all about? Does God really know or care about me?'

As I learned in my friend's apartment, God was watching out for me. His agents successfully brought me through to a place where I could not only resist the other agents, but I was able to make the decision that I was not going to play by their rules. For me, it took years to finally come to that point in my life.

So perhaps you can begin to see that if it takes so much time and effort to buy land and plan for a golf course, how much more time is needed to search our hearts and research God's Word so we can make a decision which will have eternal consequences?

With a golf course, the actual sale of the land takes place in an office far removed from the property. Once payment is made and everything is signed, the deed is given to the owner. Then and only then can it be considered theirs. Only when the price has been paid and the papers signed can the flag be raised, the mailbox put out, or the sign of ownership set up.

Nearly two thousand years ago, the price was paid for us—an act far greater than we can ever fully understand.

> *For you know that God paid a ransom to save you from the empty life you inherited from your ancestors. And the ransom He paid was not mere gold or silver. He paid for you with the precious life-blood of Christ, the sinless, spotless Lamb of God. (1 Peter 1:18–19, NLT)*

> *He brought me to the banqueting house, and his banner over me was love [for love waved as a protecting and comforting banner over my head*

12

*when I was near him]. (Song of Solomon 2:4,*
*AMP)*

## PERSONAL NOTES

_____

_____

_____

_____

_____

_____

_____

_____

_____

_____

_____

_____

# 2. The Plan

*"For I know the plans I have for you," says the Lord. "They are plans for good and not for disaster, to give you a future and a hope."(Jeremiah 29:11, NLT)*

THE LAND PURCHASED FOR A golf course is, in its present state, quite useless as such. Not until it is bought can work begin to transform it into what it is meant to be.

In a similar way, our lives have little value until we come to know and accept the truth of the great price Christ paid for us. It is part of the *fallen human condition* that we have this underlying need to be affirmed and valued. The old saying—looking for love in all the wrong places—pretty much sums it up for most of us.

It doesn't matter how good a person we are, what wonderful deeds we may do, or how hard we try, we can never *earn* God's love!

But the incredible reality is, all the love and affirmation we need, and *infinitely* more, is only a prayer away.

*When we were unable to help ourselves, at the moment of our need, Christ died for us, although we were living against God. Very few people will die to save the life of someone else. Although perhaps for a good person someone might possibly die. But God shows his great love for us in this way: Christ died for us while we were still sinners. (Romans 5:6–8, NCV)*

Imagine that the land purchased for the new golf course used to be farmland, with lots of open pastures. Perhaps it has a nice little creek and a lot of beautiful trees scattered throughout the acreage. Having grown up on a farm, I can tell you that some pastures can be cropped pretty short by the cattle or whatever livestock may be there. I can also say that I wouldn't have been the first farm lad to hit a golf ball, pretending to be on the golf course, or at the very least at the driving range. But the reality is, it isn't a golf course.

Until the land is committed into the hands of someone who can do the work needed to change it, all you have is a rough patch of real estate. Not until the papers are signed can the person with the rightful authority begin to transform the undeveloped landscape into something much more re-fined and beautiful.

This is an accurate picture of our lives. It's similar to that old phrase, a diamond in the rough. Well, that's what we all are, and there is only One who can develop us into the man or woman we were intended to be. When we accept this truth and relinquish ownership of our heart to Jesus Christ—when we ask Him to come into our hearts because we agree with God that we need Him—we are in essence signing our name to the deed along with His. It cost Him everything to offer us this deed—the very ink used is His own Blood which He shed for us!

The following verse says it all.

*For you know that God paid a ransom to save you from the empty life you inherited from your ances-tors. And the ransom he paid was not mere gold or silver. He paid for you with the precious life-blood of Christ, the sinless, spotless Lamb of God. (1 Peter 1:18–19, NLT)*

Now the Holy Spirit can to begin to transform us. God really does have a plan for our lives, and desires that we come to realize the fullness of all that He has in mind for us. The opening scripture for this chapter states this quite clearly from the book of Jeremiah.

God has plans for us.

As mentioned earlier, before construction can begin, there is much planning to be done. Contractors, architects, and consultants specifically skilled in golf-course design need to be sought out. They are the experts and there is an element of trust involved—trust in their advice and their degree of experience. Often, many candidates are interviewed until there is a decision to trust the one who seems most competent to do the job.

The Word of God even has something specific to say about this and it applies to anyone, whether they believe in God or not.

> *Without consultation, plans are frustrated, but with many counsellors they succeed. (Proverbs 15:22, NASB)*

The owner of the land may have a lot of ideas and can talk as much as they want about what it should be like, but, until the idea is finally put into the hands of those capable of bringing it forth to fruition, nothing will happen.

> *A plan in the heart of a man is like deep water, but a man of understanding draws it out. (Proverbs 20:5, NASB)*

Those architects and contractors are the *men of understanding*. Have you ever looked at the blueprints for a project and wondered how developers know what to do? I'm constantly amazed at how someone can take all they need from a piece of paper and transform that written information into a physical entity. But that's what these people are trained to do, and once they are involved and entrusted with creating the plan, work can begin. Only when the work has been committed to them can the plans be established.

The Father, Son, and Holy Spirit are our contractor, architect and consultant. They are the ones we must call upon and listen to for direction. God will guide us and He will provide all we need. As we seek Him and submit to His authority, and trust what He leads us to do, we can be sure that our lives will be changed and formed into what He wants us to be.

But, as said before, there does come a time when talking about it needs to stop and it's time to take action.

*Commit your works to the Lord, and your plans will be established. (Proverbs 16:3, NASB)*

*In all labour there is profit, but mere talk leads only to poverty. (Proverbs 14:23, NASB)*

When we invite Jesus into our lives, we know we can trust Him, even as the owner of the proposed golf course has become familiar with and trusts the qualifications of the contractor and architect. When Jesus was born in Bethlehem, his earthly father was a carpenter by trade, so He grew up learning how to build things. But His previous experience as a builder, before He came to dwell with us as a man, is much more impressive than that of a simple carpenter from Nazareth.

He is the master builder who created the heavens and the earth!

*It is I who made the earth and created mankind upon it. My own hands stretched out the heavens; I marshaled their starry hosts. (Isaiah 45:12, NIV)*

*For by him all things were created: things in heaven and on earth, visible and invisible, whether thrones or powers or rulers or authorities; all things were created by him and for him. (Colossians 1:16, NIV)*

Here is another verse that confirms that God is our *maker* and that He *knows* us.

*Before I formed you in the womb I knew you... (Jeremiah 1:5, NIV)*

It goes without saying that the landowner should be able to trust the people they've entrusted to do the job. I know that most contractors feel the same way. They want the people who hired them to rest easy and not worry.

Indeed, that sense of trust is quickly established when a true, knowledgeable professional is in charge.

Just as the contractors want their client to rest in the knowledge that they know best and are fully capable, even more so, God wants us to be able to trust Him completely with every aspect of our lives, no matter how big or small. He desires His best for us.

> *I will instruct you and teach you in the way you*
> *should go; I will counsel you and watch over you.*
> *(Psalm 32:8, NIV)*

Our heavenly Father loves it when we *ask* Him to help us understand what He is saying to us when we read something from His Word. The early disciples had Jesus with them and were able to learn from Him firsthand.

Jesus fulfilled what He came to do—to *die* for our sins. Then He rose from the grave the third day. After His resurrection, He spent a few more days with His followers, until it was time to return to heaven to be with the Father. But He promised to give the Holy Spirit to us as our teacher and counsellor.

> *And I will ask the Father, and He will give you*
> *another Counselor to be with you forever—the*
> *Spirit of Truth. (John 14:16, NIV)*

21

*"But I tell you the truth: it is for your good that I am going away. Unless I go away, the Counselor will not come to you; but if I go, I will send him to you. When he comes, He will convict the world of guilt in regard to sin and righteousness and judgment: in regard to sin, because men do not believe in Me; in regard to righteousness, because I am going to the Father, where you can see me no longer; and in regard to judgment, because the prince of this world now stands condemned.*

*"I have much more to say to you, more than you can now bear. But when he, the Spirit of truth, comes, he will guide you into all truth. He will not speak of his own; he will speak only what he hears, and he will tell you what is yet to come. He will bring glory to me by taking from what is mine and making it known to you. All that belongs to the Father is mine. That is why I said the Spirit will take what is mine and make it known to you. (John 16:7–15, NIV)*

If we are ready to trust others with our earthly plans and lean on their limited, finite wisdom, how much more should we be able to trust the all-knowing (omniscient) wisdom of the One who formed not only the earth—with us on it—but also the entire universe?

We may be able to explain the basic principles of science, but even the combined wisdom of all of mankind's greatest minds cannot explain what gives life to the tiniest cell nucleus, or understand how life itself originated.

Some accomplished people have so much education and have earned so many degrees that their business cards barely contain all the letters after their name. That might be impressive, but it's of little value next to what God knows.

The apostle Paul wrote this warning to the church at Corinth:

*Let no man deceive himself. If any man among you thinks that he is wise in this age, he must become foolish, so that he may become wise. For the wisdom of this world is foolishness before God. (1 Corinthians 3:18–19a, NASB)*

*True wisdom and power are God's. He alone knows what we should do; He understands. (Job 12:13, TLB)*

*The Lord will guide you always; He will satisfy your needs in a sun-scorched land and will strengthen your frame. (Isaiah 59:11, NIV)*

As you read these verses, how can you not begin to be comforted in the truth that we don't need to do it in our own strength or our own understanding? There are many, many-more verses from Scripture which reinforce the reality and truth of our need to trust God with every part of our lives.

If you want to meditate on and memorize God's Word, the following is a good place to start:

> *The fear of the Lord is the beginning of wisdom,*
> *and knowledge of the Holy One is understanding.*
> *(Proverbs 9:10, NIV)*

This chapter has been about how important it is to be willing to align *our plans* with *God's plan* for us. He will guide us if we ask Him, but oftentimes it can be a struggle to come to that place where we choose to let go and *let Him*.

I'll finish with these verses:

> *May He grant you according to your heart's de-sire and fulfill all your plans. We will [shout in] triumph at your salvation and victory, and in the name of our God we will set up our banners. May the Lord fulfill all your petitions. (Psalm 20:4–5, AMP)*

> *Many plans are in a man's mind, but it is the Lord's purpose for him that will stand. (Proverbs 19:21, AMP)*

*A man's mind plans his way, but the Lord directs his steps and makes them sure. (Proverbs 16:9, AMP)*

# PERSONAL NOTES

_____

_____

_____

_____

_____

_____

_____

_____

_____

_____

_____

# 3. SHAPING
# AND MOULDING

*"...Break up your fallow ground, for it is time to seek the Lord until He comes **to rain righteousness on you.**" (Hosea 10:12, NASB)*

*"The sacrifices of God are a broken spirit; a broken and contrite heart, O God, **You will not despise.**" (Psalm 51:17, NASB)*

To LOOK AT THE LAND in its natural state, one may wonder at the need for disrupting it. The natural beauty of the hills—the myriad wildflowers floating, as it were, in a sea of grasses between islands of bushy vegetation and mature trees—all taken at a glance paints a wonderful picture.

But a closer look will reveal that there is much death and decay. What looks beautiful from a distance turns out to be nothing but brambles. Wild vines are overtaking anything in their way. Even the largest and healthiest forest monarch will succumb to death as host of these prolific and leafy parasites. A drive through the country around where I live in southern Ontario (about an hour north of Toronto) quickly reveals the truth of this. Wild vines are everywhere and can be seen along a lot of the highways and side roads. In some places, they have completely covered everything and all that's left is a leafy mound as the life has been smothered from the host.

I remember, when I was young boy, there was a beautiful tree in the back bush-lot of our farm. The unique thing about this tree was the really cool vine that looped down from above and formed a natural seat that we used as a swing. I was too small to climb, but my older brothers climbed up at the right time of year and told about the grapes this vine had at the top of our huge tree.

Not too many years later, after we had moved away from the farm, I decided I wanted to find that same tree with the vine again. After much searching, I was finally able to locate it. What made it so difficult to find was the fact that the tree had died, and the vine had fallen with the tree. As a boy, I never imagined that such a big tree could ever die, but it did because the vine was thriving so much it covered the top of its host and didn't allow it to receive the life it needed from the sun.

I think the illustration here is obvious. Sin, allowed to grow unchecked in our lives, will cut us off from our source of light—Jesus, the Light of the world. And the vine that covered that tree on the farm wasn't necessarily a bad one, because it had grapes.

Even too much of something good is bad if it is allowed to come between us and God.

On the farm, the end result was death for the both the tree and the vine. When the bulk of the vine came crashing down with the dead branches that once supported it, the sudden change in location from the top of the tree to the forest floor was too much for it to adapt to. The scene that greeted me when I finally found that old tree was much less appealing than what I remembered.

The same is true with the land destined to be a golf course. Besides vines, there are coarse weeds and thistles seeking to crowd out the grasses and wildflowers. Left to itself, the land will inevitably become harsher and less attractive. I've seen many fields that once flowed with wild grasses but eventually were overgrown with thistles or some other weed not good for pasturing animals at all.

In its present state, the land is useless as a golf course. But the land now has a new owner—someone who has plans for it and who will cause it to be transformed. As the initial clearing begins, care is taken to allow the natural beauty and characteristics of the landscape to be expressed. The last thing you want to do is clear-cut everything or bulldoze the hills into flat zones.

There were lots of wonderful old trees scattered throughout the course I worked on. I was glad to see the course designer incorporate them into the areas between the fairways as the plan was being developed. It's true that in the beginning stages there were deep scars as the earth was laid bare and lots of debris was scraped away, but it was pleasing to watch as fairways were slowly moulded and carved between the hills.

That's the way it is with most golf courses. Much is uprooted and cleaned out, but only that which is in the way—only that which would block the flow of the master plan. Care is taken not to remove too many trees or to plough up too much soil. The owner and contractors watch over the work, alert to all that is happening, guiding and directing the huge machines where, and where not, to clear.

You can be sure that God is even more alert to even the smallest detail of what is happening in our lives.

As I said earlier, the land about to be changed may look beautiful as is. It's only when you take a closer look that you see the brambles and weeds, etc. Many people in the world today look like they've got it made. Jesus issues a sober warning to anyone who has grown comfortable, yet is cold towards God. Wealth can do that, although the degree of wealth that makes one comfortable certainly can vary.

Listen to this warning from Jesus:

> *But woe to you who are rich, for you have already received your comfort. (Luke 6:24, NIV)*

At a glance, everything may seem to be picture-perfect—family, house, cars, job, etc. Without exception, however, a closer look will reveal weeds and brambles—to varying degrees. Just look at all the reality TV shows starring the dysfunctional rich and famous.

*What good will it be for someone to gain the whole world, yet forfeit their soul? Or what can anyone give in exchange for their soul? (Matthew 16:26, NIV)*

*Do not store up for yourselves treasures on earth, where moth and rust destroy, and where thieves break in to steal... For where your treasure is, there your heart will be also. (Matthew 6:19, 21, NIV)*

Some weeds may be very obvious. Others, like the parasite vines, creep in and gradually choke out life. The sad part is, many do not recognize the death which is creeping through their lives.

*Their tombs will remain their houses forever, their dwelling for generations, though they had named lands after themselves.*

*Though while he lived he counted himself blessed—and men praise you when you prosper—*

*he will join the generation of his fathers, who will
never see the light of life. A man who has riches
without understanding is like the beasts that perish.
(Psalm 49:11, 18–20 NIV)*

Those are pretty strong words. Unhappy homes and broken marriages are simply interpreted as bad choices, replaceable objects, rather than being recognized as evidence of weeds of sin. The drive for position and status, and the passion for fulfilling the cravings of the flesh all testify to the need for life to have meaning, purpose and fulfillment.

Now, don't misinterpret what is being said here. Wealth and riches are not bad—it's all about how we handle it. What do we do with the wealth we attain? Do we horde it and try to get more and more, or do we use it to help others less fortunate?

*Instruct those who are rich in this present world
not to be conceited or to fix their hope on the un-
certainty of riches, but on God, Who richly sup-
plies us with all things to enjoy.*

*Instruct them to do good, to be rich in good
works, to be generous and ready to share, storing
up for themselves the treasure of a good foundation
for the future, so that they may take hold of that
which is life indeed. (1 Timothy 6:17–19, NASB)*

Solomon, the wisest man ever (second only to Jesus, of course), wrote:

*A man can do nothing better than to eat and drink and find satisfaction in his work. This too, I see, is from the hand of God, for without Him, who can eat or find enjoyment? (Ecclesiastes 2:24–25, NIV)*

The owner of the golf course wouldn't have a finished product without the planners, architects, contractors and workers. Without these people nothing would ever materialize. With the finances of the owner, these skilled people are empowered to transform the land.

As we read earlier, we have been bought, too, whether we believe it or not. Most people are quite ignorant of the role God plays in their lives. His very breath has given life to all of us! And yet the philosophy of today seeks to ignore the existence of the One true and living God. Mankind, in his arrogance, boasts that he alone has earned *this* title or built *that* empire.

God isn't fooled. He knows very well our tendencies to puff ourselves up and forget our creator, our omnipotent benefactor. His dealings with Israel throughout the Old Testament days are valuable lessons to study and learn from. We see over and over His hand guiding and providing. Look at what Moses declared to the people of Israel:

*He led you through the great and terrible wilderness, with its fiery serpents and scorpions and thirsty ground where there was no water; He brought water for you out of the rock of flint. In the wilderness He fed you manna which your fathers did not know, that He might humble you and that He might test you, to do good for you in the end. Otherwise, you may say in your heart, "My power and strength of my hand made me this wealth." But you shall remember the Lord your God, for it is He who is giving you power to make wealth... (Deuteronomy 8:15–18, NASB)*

The land, of course, has no say in who is going to buy it. But *we choose* who will be *our* owner!

*This day I call heaven and earth as witnesses against you that I have set before you life and death, blessings and curses. Now choose life, so that you and your children may live and that you may love the Lord your God, listen to His voice, and hold fast to Him. (Deuteronomy 30:19–20, NIV)*

There are two kingdoms operating in the world today. The finite and limited (relatively speaking), yet nonetheless deadly kingdom of darkness into which we all are born, and the eternal kingdom of light into which we must be born through Jesus Christ.

Jesus intercepted a young man named Saul and radically changed his life. He commissioned him to go to the gentiles and tell them the gospel message.

> ...to open their eyes and turn them from darkness to light, and from the power of Satan to God, so that they may receive forgiveness of sins and a place among those who are sanctified by faith in me. (Acts 26:18, NIV)

Imagine, if you will, that the former owner of the land refused to acknowledge that the land no longer belonged to him. In the real world that would be utterly ridiculous and with legal action would be rendered such in any court of law.

In life, as just mentioned, we have two realities operating at the same time—the physical and the spiritual. Back in the Garden of Eden, Adam relinquished his God-given authority over the earth and all that is in it to satan.

Jesus took that authority back again from satan, and has given it to us, as it was always intended. This act took place in the physical *and* the spiritual realm!

The truth that few people have understood is that *the spiritual realm is far more real than the physical world!* This world that we know will one day pass away and be destroyed, and there will be a new heaven and a new earth.

To continue with our analogy, satan is the former owner who has refused to give up ownership. The trouble is, because he is the *master of deception* and the *father of lies,* he has been able to fool us into believing that the legal rights of the new owner don't apply.

He has had a few centuries to practice on us, but you know what? He hasn't really changed his tactics much at all.

Christians, of all people, should know better, but we've been duped for so long that his lies have become second nature to us. He keeps fooling us into thinking that he has authority in our lives.

*He only has what we give him.*

When we get a cough, we *believe* that we're about to catch a cold. A worrisome ache or pain develops into a serious ailment because we *believe* that it will. The word of the doctor takes priority over the Word of God, our maker. Satan whispers—and out of forced habit—we *choose* to believe his lies.

Listen up! satan is the *defeated, dethroned,* prince of darkness. He has been defeated by Jesus Christ, *the reigning King of kings!* Jesus is the Light of the world!

*...God, the blessed and only Ruler, the King of kings and Lord of lords... (1 Timothy 6:15, NIV)*

*When Jesus spoke again to the people, he said, "I am the light of the world. Whoever follows*

*me will never walk in darkness, but will have the*
*light of life." (John 8:12, NIV)*

Jesus overcame the powers of darkness at Calvary, and yet, if we refuse to accept Him as our Lord, we remain under the authority of the kingdom of darkness. That is why there is so much evil rampant in the world today. One of the standard questions asked is, "If God is real, why is there so much evil present everywhere?"

The answer, for those who are willing to hear it, is we have abdicated our rightful, God-given authority and placed it back into the hands of the one whose sole purpose is to steal, kill, and destroy. Those who haven't yet accepted, or refuse, Jesus Christ as their Lord are still under the authority of the kingdom of darkness.

If God isn't real, why is there so much good in the world? Ever thought about it that way?

*This is the verdict: Light has come into the world,*
*but men loved darkness instead of light because*
*their deeds were evil. (John 3:19, NIV)*

*Jesus answered and said to him, "Truly, truly, I*
*say to you, unless one is born again he cannot see*
*the kingdom of God." (John 3:3, NASB)*

When we *choose* to believe and accept Jesus as our Lord and Saviour, we are *born again*. There is an interaction between the physical and the spiritual realm, and we are changed because we are moved from the kingdom of darkness into the Light.

> *But you are a chosen people, a royal priesthood,*
> *a holy nation, a people belonging to God, that*
> *you may declare the praises of him who called*
> *you out of darkness into his wonderful light.*
> *(1 Peter 2:9, NIV)*

Not everyone *feels* anything when this change of domain happens, but it is very real nonetheless. I can assure you that in the spiritual realm there *has* been a reaction. Scriptures say the angels rejoice over every soul saved. Our former master isn't unaware of what's happened either; in-fact, satan usually steps things up to try and get new believers to fall back into their old, sinful habits.

There are a number of scripture references I could use here to back that up, but instead I'll tell a story of an incident in my own life shortly after I became a born-again Christian.

I was living with my oldest brother for a few months after graduating from college. During my time at school I had become heavily involved with smoking marijuana—because that was what you did in the art programs. In an earlier chapter, I've already shared some of the process I went through in my last few months of college—the friend who tried to persuade me to go into what would've been a very destructive and degenerative lifestyle, the struggle I experienced, and how God took me out of and away from that influence.

I continued to watch the Christian television show, *The 700 Club*, whenever I could, and finally towards the end of the year (November, 1980), I prayed along with Ben, the co-host, to accept Jesus as my Lord and Saviour. And that was the point I left the kingdom of darkness and took my place in the kingdom of Light. But I can't remember *feeling* anything special—no goose bumps or tingles as such. I was alone and didn't even realize that I had become a Christian.

A change *had* taken place in me, even though I didn't feel like anything had occurred. Several weeks later, I had a strong urge to get high again, so I "borrowed" some of my brother's secret stash, sat down in the kitchen by the window, and smoked it. I still had all my drug paraphernalia—it hadn't really occurred to me to get rid of it. I still can vividly remember what happened as the effect of the drug took over me.

I was looking outside at a beautiful, sunny day. But as I came under the influence of the marijuana, everything outside became darker, as if a cloud had covered everything. I looked up and the sun was bright and the sky was clear and blue—nothing was casting a shadow, and yet *I saw* everything become shaded. At that moment a quiet voice whispered, *"I have brought you from darkness into Light."*

It startled me, even though it seemed only to be my own thoughts. It wasn't until a short time later that I read for the first time those very words in the Bible, which I quoted earlier in this chapter (1 Peter 2:9). I knew then, beyond a doubt, that the Lord had spoken to me. I gathered up my college drug stuff and threw it all in the garbage.

Satan was trying to get me back because I had made a choice to follow Christ. As a new believer, with no contact with others, I was vulnerable and susceptible to old habits. Not too long after that incident, I discovered there was a Christian drop-in centre in the same mall where I worked, and it became a wonderful place where I was able to meet other Christians and begin to grow in my faith.

Once again, God was watching out for, and leading, me.

In this chapter, I've discussed the need for the land to be changed after it has been bought. Only after it has been bought can the steps be taken to begin to clear away the debris in order to create what the new owner has in mind.

Similarly, everyone needs to come to that place where we give our lives over into the hands of God by asking Jesus into our hearts and yielding ourselves to His will for our lives. Only when we have taken that first step—out of darkness and into His Light—can He begin the real transformative work to shape and form us into what He has planned for us.

Now the work can begin within us—in our heart, our soul, and spirit. The work begins at the deepest level within us. Sometimes the outward manifestations are immediate and obvious, but changes should and will manifest more and more in every area of our lives. The key is to remain open to allow Jesus and His Holy Spirit to work in us freely.

It's not always easy. And it's not just the initial clearing away of debris that can be painful. He is still showing me areas in my life I need to yield to Him. Whatever the debris may be, it has to be removed because God truly loves us and is committed to helping us become everything He created us to be, even if it hurts.

*...because the Lord disciplines those He loves, and he punishes everyone He accepts as a son.*

*Endure hardship as discipline; God is treating you as sons. For what son is not disciplined by his father? If you are not disciplined (and everyone undergoes discipline), then you are illegitimate children and not true sons. Moreover, we have all had human fathers who disciplined us and we respected them for it. How much more should we submit to the Father of our spirits and live! Our fathers disciplined us for a little while as they thought best; but God disciplines us for our good, that we may share in his holiness. No discipline seems pleasant at the time, but painful. Later on, however, it produces a harvest of righteousness and peace for those who have been trained by it. (Hebrews 12:6–11, NIV)*

Sometimes God will, by His grace, sovereignly and instantly remove our old ways or habits, but most often it is a gradual process requiring much tearing out and uprooting of things which, if not taken out, would block God's purpose and plan from being fulfilled in us. He promises to be with us while these changes, within and without, take place.

*I will instruct you and teach you in the way you should go; I will counsel you and watch over you. (Psalm 32:8, NIV)*

*For the eyes of the Lord range throughout the earth to strengthen those whose hearts are fully committed to Him. (2 Chronicles 16:9, NIV)*

The Holy Spirit, our *comforter,* has been given to us. It is noteworthy that He is called that, because we do need a lot of tender, loving care as our lives are often turned up-side-down. He is also our counsellor and teacher, the one called alongside to help.

*But the Counselor, the Holy Spirit, whom the Father will send in my name, will teach you all things and will remind you of everything I have said to you. Peace I leave with you; my peace I give to you. I do not give to you as the world gives. Do not let your hearts be troubled and do not be afraid. (John 14:26–27, NIV)*

It truly is a beautiful assurance that we don't have to go through anything alone from now on because Jesus has promised to be with us always.

*...and surely I am with you always, to the very end of the age. (Matthew 28:20, NIV)*

*Make sure that your character is free from the love of money, being content with what you have; for He Himself has said, "I WILL NEVER DESERT YOU, NOR WILL I EVER FORSAKE YOU," so that we confidently say, "THE LORD IS MY HELPER, I WILL NOT BE AFRAID. WHAT WILL MAN DO TO ME?" (Hebrews 13:5–6, NASB)*

Through the *course* of our lives, much debris has accumulated and the tangled brambles of sin have choked the life out of different areas of our hearts. As Jesus gently and gradually cleans this all out, the light of His love shines through, causing new life to begin where darkness once was.

*For you were once darkness, but now you are light in the Lord. Live as children of light (for the fruit of the light consists in all goodness, righteousness and truth) and find out what pleases the Lord. (Ephesians 5:8–10, NIV)*

# PERSONAL NOTES

_____

_____

_____

_____

_____

_____

_____

_____

_____

_____

_____

_____

# 4. SEEDING AND FEEDING

*"Then he told them many things in parables, say-ing: 'A farmer went out to sow his seed. As he was scattering the seed, some fell along the path, and the birds came and ate it up. Some fell on rocky places, where it did not have much soil. It sprang up quickly, because the soil was shal-low. But when the sun came up, the plants were scorched, and they withered because they had no root. Other seed fell among thorns, which grew up and choked the plants. Still other seed fell on good soil, where it produced a crop—a hundred, sixty or thirty times what was sown. He who has ears, let him hear.'" (Matthew 13:3–9, NIV)*

BEFORE SEED CAN BE SOWN, there is much to be done to pre-pare the soil. It has to be cultivated, rocks and sticks need to be removed, and there may be areas where the topsoil has been scraped too thin or away completely. These areas will need to have good soil worked into them. Carefully measured and prepared mixtures of soil, seed, and fertilizer all contribute to the overall attractiveness and playability of the course.

Once seeded, care must be taken to ensure the seed is watered regularly. If the irrigation system should break down, there is danger of the seed not developing properly, possibly even dying. Much patience and perseverance is needed as daily watch is kept for signs of growth.

Have you ever planted grass seed, or any kind of seed for that matter? I have, and when I worked on the golf course, there were many times I watched areas that had been seeded and eagerly anticipated the appearance of tiny shoots. I couldn't wait for them to poke up through the soil and start to grow. Patience can wear thin, but there's nothing to do but make sure the area gets watered evenly and consistently—and wait.

Birds can be a problem, too. I've seen a flock descend and eat a seeded area so that it has to be reseeded—and that can be problem if they learn that there's fresh seed. If I remember correctly, there were some areas where the owner just gave up on seeding and laid down sod!

There is one interesting fact about seeds that is worth pondering. A dry seed unsown is quite hardy. Ancient seeds taken from tombs in pyramids have been planted after centuries of storage, and they have germinated normally.

Just add water.

But, once the seeds have germinated and the tender new shoots have begun to grow, they are very vulnerable and can die in just hours, or sooner, under a harsh sun.

Today, golf clubs are using increasingly sophisticated watering systems because owners realize that proper care and watering determines the playability, and thus the popularity, of a course. It doesn't matter how much seed is used or how excellent the quality of it, if the water isn't available to keep it growing green and healthy.

The seed in the parable of the sower, at the beginning of this chapter, represents the *Word* of God. The various soils are the differing conditions of men's hearts. Jesus was telling this parable to the disciples and went on to clearly explain what it meant.

*Hear then the parable of the sower. When any-*
*one hears the word of the kingdom and does not*
*understand it, the evil one comes and snatches*
*away what has been sown in his heart. This is*
*the one on whom seed was sown beside the road.*
*The one on whom seed was sown on the rocky*
*places, this is the man who hears the word and*
*immediately receives it with joy; yet he has no*
*firm root in himself, but is only temporary, and*
*when affliction or persecution arises because of*
*the word, immediately he falls away. And the one*

47

*on whom seed was sown among the thorns, this*
*is the man who hears the word, and the worry of*
*the world and the deceitfulness of wealth choke*
*the word, and it becomes unfruitful. And the*
*one on whom seed was sown on the good soil,*
*this is the man who hears the word and under-*
*stands it; who indeed bears fruit and brings forth,*
*some a hundredfold, some sixty, and some thirty.*
*(Matthew 13:18–23, NASB)*

Without a doubt, it is clear that much care needs to be taken to ensure proper soil conditions to receive grass seed. How much more so must our hearts be cultivated to receive God's Word? His Word will take root only if our hearts have been prepared.

In my final weeks of college, I was challenged with the state of my own heart. As I have already shared, the events leading up to the day I finally asked Jesus into my life were all part of the process of my heart being prepared. Turmoil and struggle is often part of the process of a heart being cultivated.

A few years after I became a Christian, I met someone who had been working at the college when I was a student. He had recently become a Christian as well, and shared this story. In my college days, before either of us were Christians, he was going through some rough times. I remembered speaking with him back then and, in retrospect, he did seem gruff—for lack of a better word. He explained that it was a time when God was dealing with him and bringing conviction—a time when the soil of his heart was being worked up and prepared to receive the truth of God's Word.

It's always a lot easier if we don't resist. We must openly allow God to come into every area of our hearts, to reveal and remove any sticks and stones or weeds of sin. He won't violate our free will or privacy—but we usually will lose our peace if we react stubbornly and dig in our heels.

One of the very first bible verses I memorized after I became a Christian is still good advice to this day.

*Agree with God, and be at peace; thereby good will come to you. Receive instruction from his mouth, and lay up his words in your heart. (Job 22:21–22, RSV)*

We need to yield our hearts in the same way as the writer of the following Psalms:

*Examine me, O Lord, and try me; test my heart and my mind. (Psalm 26:2, NASB)*
*Create in me a clean heart, O God, and renew a steadfast spirit within me. (Psalm 51:10, NASB)*

It would seem ludicrous to expect grass seed to germinate and grow without water to activate it and sustain its continued development. The water gives life! So, too, must the Word of God be watered regularly, once the Word of God has been planted in our hearts. This is where the analogy begins to differ a little, because God's Word is not only the seed, but also the water. We need to read His Word and allow it to take root in our spirit. As we keep reading and studying, we are strengthened and we grow.

> *For the word of God is living and active.(Hebrews 4:12, NIV)*

> *For you have been born again, not of perishable seed, but of imperishable, through the living and enduring word of God. (1 Peter 1:23, NIV)*

God's Word is living and active! It is *alive!* It is the *nourishment* of our spirit! This is not a figure of speech—it is reality. By His Holy Spirit, as we read His Word, the living, active life thereof permeates our spirit and releases life-giving strength and nourishment within us. There is a reason why it is referred to as the *bread of life*. It is, or should be, our daily bread, even as we need food for our bodies every day.

The more we are open and yielded to learn and receive from His Word, the more we will absorb it into the soil of our hearts.

The Word of God is divinely *alive* with *power.*

Someone once used the analogy of an invisible faucet. The more we look into God's Word to study and learn from it, the more the faucet is opened and the greater the flow of *living water*.

One thing is sure: the living, active, life-giving power of the Word will always flow to the one whose heart is inclined to learn from it!

It is important to understand, even if the person doesn't feel they are gaining anything, it doesn't mean they aren't. Just as it appears nothing is happening when seed is put in the ground, we know by faith that it will germinate and grow.

Ours is not a walk based on what we can see or feel—it is one of faith.

*For we walk by faith, not by sight. (2 Corinthians 5:7, NASB)*

When Jesus explained the meaning of the parable of the sower, he referred to *the evil one* who came to steal away the seed. Stealing is just part of what he does. We learn from scripture that the devil is the *deceiver* of the world.

*And the great dragon was thrown down, the serpent of old who is called the devil and Satan, who deceives the whole world; he was thrown down to the earth, and his angels were thrown down with him. (Revelation 12:9, NASB)*

Deception is his greatest tool, yet, we need to learn this basic fact—***the devil has been defeated!***

Through and in Christ, we have been given power and authority over the enemy and his entire dark kingdom. Listen to what Jesus said when the disciples returned from a time on the road ministering in His name.

> *And the seventy returned with joy, saying, "Lord, even the demons are subject to us in Your name." And He said to them, "I was watching Satan fall from heaven like lightning. Behold, I have given you authority to tread upon serpents and scorpions, and over all the power of the enemy, and nothing shall injure you. Nevertheless do not rejoice in this, that the spirits are subject to you, but rejoice that your names are recorded in heaven."*
> *(Luke 10:17–20, NASB)*

Jesus made it very clear, on more than one occasion, that we have nothing to fear from the powers of darkness. By dying on the cross and taking our sins upon Himself, He broke any binding legalities satan may have held over us. One of the final statements He made to the disciples, just before he ascended into heaven, was this:

> *All authority has been given to Me in heaven and*
> *on earth....and lo, I am with you always, even to*
> *the end of the age. (Matthew 28:18, 20, NASB)*

Therefore, when we ask Jesus into our hearts, we have the assurance of His ever-present help. We have been given all authority, too, as followers of Christ. In Jesus' name, we have the legal right to overturn and nullify any work of the evil one. But we need to do as Jesus did, and ask the Father for direction. There may be specific keys for release we need to pray about, such as forgiveness to free us from the bondage of *unforgiveness*; people have to make choices, but generally speaking, it doesn't matter whether it is sickness, oppression or disease—we have the authority!

> *...because greater is He who is in you than he*
> *who is in the world. (1 John 4:4, NASB)*

This one basic, profound truth is what satan works hardest to deceive and keep people from learning.

We should realize then, as we read the Word, if we *feel* we are gaining nothing, this is contrary to what we know by faith about God's Word. As we read or listen to it with an open, teachable heart, our spirit *is* being fed and strengthened in the flow of living water—even if we don't feel it to be so.

This is where discipline is so important. Just as grass seed needs care on a daily basis, even more so do we need to study the Word of God every day, even if only for a few minutes. We must keep the faucet open and the flow continuing. Each time we give in to the subtle schemes and whisperings of the deceiver and begin to avoid time in the Word of God, we rob ourselves of the life which comes from His Word into our spirit. Soon the *feeling* will become reality, as our dry, thirsty spirit cries out for nourishment. But, if we maintain disciplined study, persevering through dry times, eventually the deception of dryness will be replaced with cascading fountains and deep reservoirs of living water—rivers springing up from within us, flowing—unable to be contained or hidden by the lies of a *defeated* foe!

> *...but whoever drinks the water I give him will never thirst. Indeed, the water I give him will become in him a spring of water welling up to eternal life. (John 4:14, NIV)*

So, we know it takes faith to plant grass seed (or any kind of seed) and expect it to sprout and grow into what it is supposed to be. The right amount of water and warm sunshine work together with faith to bear fruit.

First, we need to receive God's gift of salvation, and then we begin to learn to appropriate His truths throughout scripture. Through faith, we can experience growth in every area of our lives by learning to persevere with joy, through every trial and testing, knowing His Word will not fail. But, in order for us to see good fruit in our lives, we need to have a good mixture of the water of His Word *and* times of basking in the sunshine of His presence. When we do this we are not just being *watered*, we are allowing the water to enable the seed to germinate and grow. We need those times to allow our spirits and our faith to be strengthened. We will be like the person in the parable of the seeds who received the Word with understanding. If we can manage this kind of disciplined lifestyle, we can expect to live victorious and fruitful lives.

So many people, Christians included, are bound to all kinds of sicknesses and snares of the enemy, simply because we do not know (or believe) what God's Word says about it, or about us. We believe the lies satan tells us, rather than looking to what God has to say in His Word.

Some people will have difficulty receiving that truth, especially pastors and ministers. How can you preach that God heals when the people you pray for don't get healed? Fortunately, more and more people are coming to their senses and are repenting of watering down the full gospel simply to keep from looking like failures when someone isn't healed immediately through prayer. Many times, the blame has been put on the person who is asking for prayer. That couldn't be further from the truth.

I have heard many testimonies of people who wanted to move out of the rut of religiosity and begin to move in the supernatural power of God with signs and wonders. They would begin to pray for people who needed healing, but in most cases, there wasn't a lot of evidence of answered prayer, at least, not until weeks or even months later. I believe that it was a time of testing them to see if they would continue to stand firm and persevere, regardless of what they saw, or didn't see, happening. In every story, those who hung in and refused to give up finally broke through whatever invisible barrier had been there, and they began to experience and witness the power of God move when they prayed.

Maybe it's the enemy who causes the delays, but you can be sure God is watching and waiting to see if we really do believe, or if we're going to give up.

I believe it is all part of testing us to see if we will choose the lies of the enemy or press on and in to appropriate the truth clearly stated in God's Word. And that takes a lot of effort! How many of us are truly willing to *pray* the price!

I have heard more than one testimony of someone who has had a vision of heaven, and has seen a large room or warehouse full of body parts. That sounds gruesome at first, to be sure, but then it was explained that these are for the people who need new limbs, or whatever is needed. If only the *church* would pray harder, they would receive.

It has been too easy to make excuses. Fortunately, in our weakness and unbelief, God can still cause us to grow. Indeed, I do believe that some sickness and disease is divinely appointed to teach us valuable lessons and to turn our hearts to God, but I tend to think that is usually only a last resort on His part.

The apostle Paul had a physical ailment he describes as a *thorn in the flesh* which he prayed three times for God to remove. God refused and instead told him that His strength is perfected in weakness. Why is that? Some have suggested that it helped to keep Paul humble and remind Him that his strength comes from God, not his own abilities, spiritual gifts, or ministry.

I have had a problem with my stomach all my life. The valve at the top doesn't work properly, so I've always had problems with acid reflux. It is something I have asked to be healed, but in the meantime, I can see how God has used it for good. Something I carried over from my days before I was a Christian was the tendency to drink more alcohol than I should when I have been depressed, angry, or stressed. The pain from my stomach has been a faithful reminder to stop and get things in my life straightened out with God. Fortunately, that is only a last resort, and over the years I have learned to heed and respond to the Holy Spirit without always having to be disciplined through the pain of my own spiritual negligence.

Like grass kept in the dark and not watered, we will grow pale and weak if we do not spend time in the Word. This is evident in all walks of life, with people who do not know God (perhaps your neighbour), but is most plainly seen in the faces of people in the inner cities or in most of the impoverished third-world countries. Whenever one of

these souls is exposed to the love of God and opens to receive that love and what His Word says, the transformation
is usually remarkable. It is truly the testimony of the *life* to
be found when a heart receives Christ and begins to learn
and study His Word.

When our spirits are renewed and strengthened by the
Holy Spirit, our bodies are strengthened, too.

*The spirit sustains the physical!*

When I was a new believer, the Holy Spirit spoke this
truth into my heart. Our spirit, soul and body are insepa-
rable and yet uniquely different and distinct.

When our spirit is weak, our body is more susceptible
to sickness. The food of our spirit is God's Word. It's as
simple as that.

We are also strengthened in spirit simply by taking
the time to wait before Him quietly. Worship and praise is
also crucial—perhaps the most important habit we could
ever develop.

> *He gives strength to the weary, and to him who
> lacks might He increases power. Though youths
> grow weary and tired, and vigorous young men
> stumble badly, yet those who wait for the Lord
> will gain new strength; They will mount up with
> wings like eagles, they will run and not get tired,
> they will walk and not become weary. (Isaiah
> 40:29–31, NASB)*

In the analogy of the grass seed, I observed how easily the new shoots can be damaged, once the seed has germinated and begun to grow. I shared briefly in the last chapter that, not too long after I knew I was a Christian, I eventually found a Christian drop-in centre where I was surrounded by other believers and I was able to attend Bible studies. I found a church and started attending, and I really began to grow, just like a good seed in good soil.

I was alone when I first prayed the prayer of salvation. I didn't know that *Christian* was the word commonly used to describe what I now was. I know that may seem odd, but at least I knew I was *saved*.

Remember how the newly sprouted seed is so vulnerable if it isn't cared for? Our enemy, satan, would like nothing more than to destroy that new life. I was in a very vulnerable position, because my involvement with destructive drug habits during college had given satan legal authority in certain areas of my life. When I prayed and asked Jesus Christ to be Lord of my life, He became the new owner because He paid for my sins and died in my place on the cross.

But satan doesn't give up easily. He had failed to keep me from becoming a Christian, but he knew I didn't know very much about anything, so he changed his tactics. He whispered to me that since I really believed in heaven, why not avoid all the hassles of the future and just *check in* early? He may have lost my soul, but now he wanted to keep me from *living* my life for God and doing anything for God.

That's why I went for a drive one bright, winter afternoon, just weeks after being born again. My objective was to find an isolated country road, back my little car into a snow bank, leave the car running and let the exhaust fumes overwhelm me. I can still remember my line of reasoning at the time: life seemed to hold too many challenges that just didn't seem worth the trouble, so, since I was assured that heaven was real, why not just go there now—rather sooner than later! I wasn't feeling depressed or sad. It just seemed an expedient thing to do. Fortunately for me, every time I thought I had found a quiet enough road with a good snow bank, a car would come along. After driving around for about an hour, I finally began to realize it wasn't going to happen, so decided to give up.

Just then I heard a still, small voice within me say something like, *"I have work for you to do."* I knew that it wasn't my own thoughts speaking. My response was something simple like, "Oh." I didn't know what else to say, but I knew what I had heard. I then drove around a while longer and simply enjoyed the scenery because it was, after all, a beautiful winter afternoon.

Many things on a golf course can damage grass, whether it's newly planted or old sod. People are easily scarred, too, some wounds being very deep and traumatic. It doesn't matter if the wounds occur before we are saved or after; they still need to be healed. With the proper care and maintenance (prayer and ministry), even the deepest scar can be fixed by someone who knows how to do it properly.

There are many excellent books found in Christian bookstores (or online) which deal extensively with the relationship of spirit, soul and body. They illustrate more clearly than I can here how we can be wounded and how God can heal. There is, however, one profound truth which I've learned:

*True worship heals all wounds!*

When we worship with total abandonment of heart we will find ourselves, our *spirits,* in the presence of God. God says that He inhabits the praises of His people. In His presence we are healed. In His presence we are changed.

In summary, this chapter has been about seeds and caring for or feeding that seed. I hope that the analogy has been clear how it applies to us and our relationship with God and His Word. Scripture is our source of Truth. We do need to pray for understanding, though, and not be like those God spoke about through the prophet Hosea.

*My people are destroyed for lack of knowledge. (Hosea 4:6, NASB)*

*So faith comes from hearing, and hearing by the word of Christ. (Romans 10:17, NASB)*

*I said, "Plant the good seeds of righteousness, and you will harvest a crop of love. Plow up the hard ground of your hearts, for now is the time*

*to seek the LORD, that he may come and shower*
*righteousness upon you." (Hosea 10:12, NLT)*

# PERSONAL NOTES

_____

_____

_____

_____

_____

_____

_____

_____

_____

_____

_____

_____

# 5. Washouts

*"Do not rejoice over me, O my enemy. Though
I fall I will rise; Though I dwell in darkness, the
LORD is a light for me." (Micah 7:8, NASB)*

Washouts can be very discouraging in the development
of a golf course, and in the life of a Christian. On a newly
seeded course, too much water can cause soil to become
saturated. Consequently, mudslides will remove not only
the seed but huge amounts of precious topsoil. This usually
happens when there is a storm, but also might be the result
of the watering system left on too long. Both of these events
happened on the golf course I was working on.

Washouts may happen often, but the owner doesn't
give up and forget the whole idea of having a golf course,
because it isn't the whole course which is damaged; most
of the course is developing well. Instead, attention is given
to those areas that need repair. As the roots grow deeper,

the grass thickens until nothing short of an earthquake can move it.

New Christians are most vulnerable to discouraging failures because there are areas in their heart where God's Word has not yet reached or taken root. They may *wash out* in the same destructive habit over and over, but giving up the idea of being a Christian isn't the answer.

The golf course I worked on was very hilly, which made it quite a challenge to get seed to grow before it washed away. One area had a major washout after a rainstorm. It left a ravine several feet wide and deep, stretching across more than one fairway. I mean, we had to haul in a *lot* of dirt to fill it up, and then we had to plant seed again. The problem was, because of the natural layout of the hills, the washout was where the water focused its descent to the lower levels of the valley. The rest of the golf course had only minor damage here and there, but this was a big one— and it was springtime. The next big rainstorm, after we had worked very hard filling it in and reseeding, it washed out again just as deep. The new soil soaked up more water than it could hold and there was nothing to hold it back. We definitely had a serious problem. I can't remember exactly what the owners did to fix it, but I think it involved ditches, culverts, and lots of sod.

By the end of the summer you would never have known there had been a problem. It had been discouraging to us, who had to look at it up close and deal with it, but the owners had seen the bigger picture and we patiently worked on the problem areas until they were no longer an issue.

That's the way we need to approach problems in our lives, too. We know we must be disciplined in our reading and studying of the bible, but just as grass seed can receive too much water, we too need time to allow what we have heard and read to not only soak in, but to become well-rooted in our heart. God often just wants us to sit quietly in His presence.

*Cease striving (relax) and know that I am God.*
*(Psalm 46:10, NASB)*

Even as I write this, I am acutely aware of the need to do this myself, but the ability to simply *do it* is frustratingly evasive. God promises us that as we take time to just be alone with Him, He will come to us.

*My God in His lovingkindness will meet me.*
*(Psalm 59:10, NASB)*

He loves us and speaks to us and causes us to be re-newed and strengthened in our inner self, our spirit. It is in these times of quiet fellowship with Him that our *roots* grow deeper in Him, especially if we're in the middle of a *washout*. When we don't spend this kind of quality time with Him, we can easily lose our perspective and allow the enemy room to spread weeds of confusion in our minds.

65

One thing can lead to another and an area of weakness surfaces. If we have a *washout*, instead of going to God and talking to Him about it, we often—for a host of reasons—keep it to ourselves and try to work it out alone. The danger is that we focus on the area of weakness to the exclusion of all the other places where there has been good development and growth. This is why it's good to have people around us we can trust enough to talk to and pray with—people who can encourage us. Encouragement is a powerful thing. We all need to be encouraged, because it helps to shift our focus off the negative.

Another thing I've discovered to be a problem is listening to too much teaching without putting what I've learned into action. It's like getting watered until we are saturated and can't receive any more.

When I first became a Christian, I was at church every Sunday morning, eager to listen to the Word of God being preached. I went to another church Sunday evenings for their late service because my church didn't have one. I went to Tuesday-night bible study, and Friday night I was at a drop-in centre for the youth group study time. Now, exposure to all this teaching was okay because two things were happening. One, all of the teaching from God's Word was not only watering what had already been planted in my heart, but it was helping to plant more seed in me. Just as newly planted seed needs a lot of water, so did I, and I was certainly getting it. Two, I was involved in other church and community activities where I was serving. I was, in essence, putting into practice what I was learning, and doing that helped the seed being sown in my heart to take deeper root. That's what obedience to the Word of God does—it makes the roots go deeper. My focus was on the needs of others. Isn't that the basic message of Christ—to be a servant?

Somewhere along the way, though, I *served* less but I continued to attend and receive wonderful teaching from church, at seminars and conferences, etc. After a while it all became tiresome and I didn't have the same enthusiasm. I eventually realized that the problem wasn't with the teachers or the content of the teaching, but it was me. I was overwatered—saturated.

This can be a dangerous place to be in. The enemy can come in and deceive us in many ways if we are not careful. Before we know it, we can become overly focused on an area in our lives that we know needs to be changed, or worse, we can start to focus on someone else's perceived shortcomings. The negative becomes the primary focus and we forget about the positive. It becomes an area of introspection and we can really begin a rapid downward spiral spiritually. Fortunately, God knows what's going on with us and is more than capable of bringing us back to the balance of listening, learning, and serving.

We must realize that God will allow us to be tested so we can grow deeper roots and become stronger *in Christ*.

*Consider it pure joy, my brothers, whenever you
face trials of many kinds, because you know that
the testing of your faith develops perseverance.
...Blessed is the man who perseveres under trial,
because when he has stood the test, he will receive the crown of life that God has promised to
those who love him. (James 1:2–3, 12, NIV)*

*And not only this, but we also exult in our tribu-
lations, knowing that tribulation brings about
perseverance; and perseverance, proven character; and proven character, hope; and hope
does not disappoint, because the love of God has
been poured out within our hearts through the
Holy Spirit who was given to us. (Romans 5:3–5,
NASB)*

*And He has said to me, "My grace is sufficient for
you, for power is perfected in weakness." Most
gladly, therefore, I will rather boast about my
weakness, that the power of Christ may dwell in
me. (2 Corinthians 12:9, NASB)*

Five years after I became a Christian, I found myself
living and working at a retreat centre about an hour north
of Toronto, Canada. It was a perfect place for me to *grow*

because I was able to sit in on most of the teaching courses, but at the same time I was able work and serve the guests that continually came and went. I remember one late winter day, as I was out on the property, I looked down the valley and felt such an incredible sense of peace and belonging. I knew beyond any doubt that this was where God wanted me to be.

It couldn't have been much more than a month later that I was asked to come to the office, where it was explained that they felt it was time for me to move on. The real reason was finances—a constant concern for ministries that rely on donations to keep operating. Fortunately, I was able to keep living there, but it was necessary for me to look for employment elsewhere. I took the opportunity to apply to Youth with a Mission (YWAM), and I was accepted into their five-month program that was due to start in the fall. That was a good thing, because it gave me something to aim for at the end of the summer.

In the meantime, I didn't realize how deeply I had been hurt or just how much rejection had been stirred up within me as a result of that little meeting in the spring. Part of me was very angry, because I didn't believe they had heard from God. I felt it was a manmade decision, but there was nothing to do except trust that God would bring good out of it. Still, as the summer went by, the anger and rebellion simmered quietly and seeped out little by little. I began going out to bars with one of the fellows on the construction site who I had become friends with. On the one hand, I really tried to witness to him, but on the other, I began to drink more and began to go to places by myself that I shouldn't have. By the end of the summer, I was even offered some marijuana, which I tried. It was the first time back to that old habit since the time in my brother's apartment, shortly after I had become a Christian. I still remembered what God had spoken to me back then, but over the past few weeks I had allowed myself to become so focused on the negative that I had no interest in serving God or doing anything for Him.

Somewhere along the way I had transferred all my disappointments and anger, all of my negative feelings, to God. I wasn't about to renounce my faith, but I surely wasn't going to go out of my way to work for Him.

Meanwhile, there was a lady who would often pray for and minister to the staff at the retreat centre. She was, I believe, one of God's Generals and she moved powerfully in the Spirit when she prayed for people. She had promised to take time at some point over the summer to pray with me, but, as each week went by, the appointment kept getting put off. Little did she know that this just fuelled and reinforced the rejection I felt at the time.

September came, and I had reached a critical point in my walk as a Christian. The prayer and ministry I had been promised, and which I was very much aware I needed, still hadn't happened. In fact, it didn't look like it would at all, because the lady was scheduled to leave for western Canada to visit her family.

Two things happened, which not only changed that, but really confirmed that God was very much aware of my needs. The lady suddenly felt an urgent prompt from the Lord to set aside time for me before she went on her trip. When she came and met with me, I was able to share with her a dream I just had, which confirmed why the Lord didn't want her to delay.

In my dream, I was standing on the very brink of a cliff. The bottom could not be seen, but the next step in that direction would have caused me to fall into oblivion. That was a very clear picture of where I was spiritually, but God, in His faithfulness, didn't allow that to happen. I was prayed for and ministered to deeply. I was even assured by the Lord that He understood how I felt and that even though I had done things I shouldn't have, I was not only forgiven, but fully restored. What should've been a devastating washout in my life had been averted and I was able to carry on knowing that He truly loved me and was watching over me. Those assurances effectively silenced any guilt or condemnation that the enemy would have tried to speak into me.

Failure is part of maturing. We must not let ourselves become lax, but neither are we to let ourselves be overcome with guilt. The enemy would love to steal our joy by speaking condemnation and accusations to us, and to God. We must realize that a major part of the enemy's tactic is to lay guilt on us. He is very legalistic and is always looking for something to hold up at us and say, "See, you failed here—

you did this and said that; If you were a true Christian you wouldn't be like this. You should just give up. Nobody likes a hypocrite." This accusing voice can come at us from within our own head or from people around us, which can be even more hurtful.

We need to look at what John wrote in the book of Revelation:

> *Then I heard a loud voice in heaven, saying, "Now the salvation, and the power, and the kingdom of our God and the authority of His Christ have come, for the accuser of our brethren has been thrown down, who accuses them before our God day and night." (Revelation 12:10, NASB)*

Another thing to realize is that it is not a sin to be tempted. It's how we respond that determines if we resist or give in to the temptation, and therefore sin. Jesus was tempted, but He did not sin.

> *Then Jesus was led by the Spirit into the desert to be tempted by the devil. (Matthew 4:1, NIV)*

For anyone not familiar with this account, it goes on to tell how the devil appeared and tempted Jesus with specific things, and he even quoted scripture. Each time, there was some immediate benefit Jesus could have gained (like bread from a stone—after forty days without food, you know that would have tempting), but Jesus also responded with the Word of God, accurately using scripture to expose the attempts of the devil to trick Him.

Most often, the devil will appeal to our fleshly desires and appetites, just the way he did with Jesus. The enemy's tactics haven't changed much since back then, although in this modern day and age there are certainly a wider variety of enticements. It's also interesting and valuable for us to recognize the determination of the enemy. The account of Jesus being tempted in the wilderness ends by saying that when the devil had finished every temptation, he departed until an *opportune time.*

Not only do we need to know God's Word, we need to be obedient and apply it daily, and yield our wills and desires by learning what His will and desire is for us. Then we can effectively and successfully resist the enemy when he comes at us.

> *Submit therefore to God. Resist the devil and he*
> *will flee from you. (James 4:7, NASB)*

That verse may seem small, but it really does work. Jesus showed us that it works. His whole life is the perfect example for us to follow.

> *Although He was a Son, He learned obedience*
> *from the things which He suffered. And having*

*been made perfect, He became to all those who obey Him the source of eternal salvation. (Hebrews 5:8–9, NASB)*

*And being found in appearance as a man, He humbled Himself by becoming obedient to the point of death, even death on a cross. (Philippians 2:8, NASB)*

Because of all Jesus suffered for us, He has made it possible for us to look to Him for help whenever we feel tempted, or even when we have had a washout.

*For since He Himself was tempted in that which He suffered, He is able to come to the aid of those who are tempted. (Hebrews 2:18, NASB)*

*Hence, also, He is able to save forever those who draw near to God through Him, since He always lives to make intercession for them. For it was fitting that we should have such a high priest, holy, innocent, undefiled, separated from sinners and exalted above the heavens... (Hebrews 7:25–26, NASB)*

Through Christ we can be free of all guilt. While the Holy Spirit will *convict* us of any sin that needs to be dealt with, the devil will take it before God to argue for legal ground to afflict and torment us. We need to be sensitive to the voice of our *counsellor* given us from above and *quick* to repent of any sin *before* the enemy has a chance to use it against us. Even when we do, he may still try to rub our face in it. The following verse will silence the voice of the accuser, if we believe it.

> *If we confess our sins, He is faithful and righteous to forgive us our sins and to cleanse us from all unrighteousness. (1 John 1:9, NASB)*

When we do this sincerely, our relationship with God is renewed and strengthened, and our accuser is *silenced!*

> *There is therefore now no condemnation for those who are in Christ Jesus. (Romans 8:1, NASB)*

There will always be times of stumbling in our walk with Jesus, just as there will always need to be repairs to the golf course. But even as the golf course matures and the grass is able to grow its roots deep, so too, as long as we are allowing the seed of God's Word to be planted and nourished, as long as our hearts are *truly seeking* God's way and we are not *consciously harbouring* any sinful way, we can be assured that God will keep and sustain us daily.

*The steps of a man are established by the Lord; and He delights in his way. When he falls he shall not be hurled headlong; because the Lord is the One who holds his hand. (Psalm 37:23–24, NASB)*

*For the righteous man falls seven times, and rises again... (Proverbs 24:16, NASB)*

How bitter the tears can be over some failures—and as we weep, the enemy laughs. We must see him as nothing more than a tool in the hand of God. Our heavenly Father allows hidden sins to be uprooted and brought to the surface so He can work a deeper healing in us. He only wants to remove that which would eventually destroy us if allowed to remain. Consequently, we may go through dark valleys, because attention is focused on the circumstances or situation. As we seek God's face and lay our hearts open to His love, as we earnestly humble ourselves before Him, we will receive grace to repent, to forgive, to love—grace for whatever is needed.

*But as for me, I will watch expectantly for the Lord; I will wait for the God of my salvation. My God will hear me. Do not rejoice over me, O my enemy. Though I fall I will rise; though I dwell in darkness, the Lord is a light for me. (Micah 7:7–8, NASB)*

*My soul, wait in silence for God only, for my hope is in Him. He only is my rock and my salvation, my stronghold; I shall not be shaken. On God my salvation and my glory rest; the rock of my strength, my refuge is in God. Trust in Him at all times, O people; Pour out your heart before Him; God is a refuge for us. Selah. (Psalm 62:5–8, NASB)*

# PERSONAL NOTES

# 6. Ready for Use

*"Arise, shine; for your light has come, and the glory of the Lord has risen upon you. For behold, darkness will cover the earth, and deep darkness the peoples; but the Lord will **rise upon you, and His glory will appear upon you. And nations will come to your light, and kings to the brightness of your rising."** (Isaiah 60:1–3, NASB)*

As we have seen, making a golf course requires a considerable investment and commitment of time and money. The opening day is, therefore, impatiently anticipated as the final stages of preparation are put in place. The course is really beginning to look like it's ready to be played, so it's hard not to want to get out there on it and, from the owner's perspective, to start making some money. To compare it now to what it started from testifies to the immense changes that have occurred. I would sometimes stand at the fence between the new golf course and the property next to it and think how it all used to look the same. But now, the neighbouring land appears all the more wild next to groomed and manicured hills which were just as untamed not very long ago.

This is a crucial time, because care must be taken to allow the new grass to take hold firmly. Patience is needed until it is mature enough to be used and enjoyed for what it has been created. The roots must go deep to withstand the surface traffic to come. If opened to play too soon, much damage could occur, causing a greater delay and potentially a negative reputation.

This is exactly what happened on the course I worked on. In the summer of the year it was being built, the owners decided to open it up, even though the grass had not grown in on many of the greens or in areas of the fairways. In fairness, I can't blame them for being so eager to show off the course but, as one who worked on it, I saw how much more work it required to make unnecessary repairs—all because of impatience. Fortunately, many years have passed since then and it has developed into a beautiful, mature course. Anybody who may have had a bad round of golf during that first year has no doubt been back to experience it in its prime, but I used to wonder if any were simply put off enough that they didn't bother to try it again.

One of the most common faults we have today is impatience. Christians are very much guilty of this as well. In this modern world of fast food and instant everything, we have difficulty conforming to God's timetable. God wants us to learn to trust Him. He knows *what* we need and *when* we need it, and there are many scriptures which encourage us to redirect our focus.

> *Trust in the Lord, and do good; dwell in the land and cultivate faithfulness. Delight yourself in the Lord; and He will give you the desires of your heart. Commit your way to the Lord, trust also in Him and He will do it. He will bring forth your righteousness as the light, and your judgment as the noonday. (Psalm 37:3–6, NASB)*

Sometimes, new Christians may accept, or have put on them, responsibilities which they are not yet ready for. It might be something God is preparing them for, but they rush ahead too soon. God's Word needs time to take root and become firmly established, or else we will be like the golf course which is opened prematurely and suffers physical damage, as well as a negative reputation. This is the kind of snare the enemy can use to cause much confusion and pain. In fact, there can be deadly consequences if we haven't learned to wait for God's timing. Immaturity and impatience don't allow us to discern the leading of the Holy Spirit. People have too often rushed ahead of the Lord, to the detriment of their own health and sometimes the loss of life. All of it is observed by non-Christians, who are quick to pick up on the failures of Christians—especially those in leadership. Our lives are meant to draw people to God, not drive them away.

This was something Christians had to deal with in the early days of the church. Look at what the Apostle Paul had to say to Timothy, who was trying to appoint overseers and deacons over a new fellowship:

> *An elder must not be a new believer, because he might become proud, and the devil would cause him to fall...Before they are appointed as deacons, let them be closely examined. If they pass the test, then let them serve as deacons. (1Timothy 3:6, 10, NLT)*

I knew such a man. He became a Christian through a move of God in the inner city of Toronto in the mid 1970s. Almost immediately, he was made a deacon. He ended up renting a house with others from this same fellowship, and became the overseer of it. In time, most of the people moved on with their lives, and it was a little later that I came to live there, along with two or three other young men. I soon discerned that he had a lot of spiritual pride. Even though I was a new believer, I recognized this pride because it was very unmistakable. Eventually, I had had enough of the religious ranting, and confronted him.

In those days, being new in the ways of Christianity, I didn't have the *gentleness of wisdom* that the book of

James describes, and so the resulting confrontations we had were very loud and animated, to say the least. After a few months, I left the house to live elsewhere, too, but in later conversations with him he confessed that he did grow from those confrontations.

I'd like to think I've matured in that area of my life, because the tendency to confront and not back down is still there. I have gotten better, but I know it's still something I need to work on. All of us have aspects of our personality that can be abrasive, for lack of a better word. But that doesn't mean it's a bad quality. Like the analogy of a diamond in the rough, when we give our lives over into God's hands, He can take any *abrasive* characteristic and smooth it into something bold and strong—tempered with His love and gentleness.

Waiting on God is not something to be taken lightly. We need to spend time with our heavenly Father every day, speaking to Him and *listening* to Him. We do this by reading His Word, and as we read we need to ask Him to reveal His truths to us and help us to *understand* what we are reading. As we do, we will grow to know His voice, and His will, more clearly.

I listened to the testimony of a man recently who told several stories that clearly illustrated just how important it is to discern and be obedient to the voice of God. He told how he had been leading a team of believers on a prayer mission to another country, where Christianity was not allowed. Near the end of their time, they learned of a flight which would take them out a day early. It was very appealing, because the heat was unbearable and they were tired, sweaty and dirty. The other option was a very long, uncomfortably hot bus ride. He declined the plane because he was told by the Lord he would be in that country for so many days, and no more, no less.

The other members of his team were not too happy to stay and endure the heat and a long bus trip, but they quickly changed their tune afterwards when they learned that the plane they had wanted to take had crashed, killing all on board. And this was just one of many such stories he had. If he had been a new Christian, he probably would have gone along with the others, got on that early plane, and they all would have lost their lives. He had learned how to listen to and discern the leading of the Holy Spirit through years of practice.

*I will instruct you and teach you in the way you should go; I will instruct you with My eye upon you. (Psalm 32:8, NASB)*

*Make me know Your ways, O LORD; Teach me Your paths. Lead me in Your truth and teach me,*

*For You are the God of my salvation; For You I wait all the day. (Psalm 25:4–5, NASB)*

*Rest in the Lord and wait patiently for Him.*
*(Psalm 37:7, NASB)*

As I mentioned earlier in this chapter, waiting is one of the hardest things for any of us to do in this day of instant everything. The owners of the golf course I worked at couldn't wait for the grass to grow in before they opened it up to be used—but, over the course of time, everything did grow in and all is well. Fortunately, God does extend grace to cover our shortcomings.

I remember hearing the story of a pastor in northern Ontario who went to visit an elderly man who was very sick in bed. He took with him a man who had recently become a Christian and was very zealous for the things of God. This new Christian had just read how one of the Old Testament prophets had raised a boy from the dead by laying on top of the body. Before the pastor knew what was happening, this very large, burly man threw himself on top of the frail old man and commanded him to be healed in the name of Jesus. By God's grace, the old guy not only wasn't injured, but he was indeed healed.

Even new Christians can do mighty works for the Lord. There is no reason not to expect that to happen. As they receive God's Word into their hearts, they need to act and begin to use their newfound faith.

Or, as someone once put it, we need to *act*—in order to *activate*—our faith. The more we do, the faster we'll grow—as long as we keep being fed and watered regularly from God's Word.

Just as grass grows faster and greener when it is fertilized and watered, so we will mature as Christians the more we feed upon His Word, bask in His glorious presence, *and* put into practice what we learn.

> *I wait for the Lord, my soul waits, and in His Word I do hope. (Psalm 130:5, NASB)*

During my first five years as a new believer, as I described earlier, I went to church twice on Sunday, attended mid-week bible study, and joined a Friday night youth group. There were often other activities on other days or evenings that I found myself involved with, too. I remember people saying to me how I seemed to be very mature for a young believer. It was very encouraging to me, because I certainly didn't feel like I was. It helped me to see that there are many ways our lives can glorify God, whatever stage we're at, as we are growing up spiritually. Hopefully, anyone should be able to see considerable changes in us now, compared to what we were like before we invited Jesus into our hearts. It's just like comparing the finished golf course with the nearby field that it once was part of—the difference is unmistakable.

For me, the changes may not have been as outwardly dramatic as some, but there were clear changes, such as not hanging out with the same friends who I used to drink with or do drugs with while in college. My interest in that old way of life was gone completely. The real changes happening in me were deeper, inside my heart.

Patience has not been one of my strongest virtues, to say the least. While I have been encouraged to know that I have been growing, I have often been impatient. I have always felt there is more that God has for me to do—a greater calling, so to speak. I've always been frustrated at not moving in the same power and authority as the early church. The first chapters of the book of Acts give good examples of how we should be today.

However, I have come to realize that there has been much that God has needed to do in and with me over the years. I know from experience that when we try using His authority, the enemy will challenge and attack us where we are weakest. That's why it is essential that we have enough maturity as believers to know what to do. If we're going to take a swing at the enemy, we need to be firmly anchored to the Rock. We really need to have a disciplined life of prayer and fellowship with our God and Father. Only God can heal or restore those areas within us that need His touch, and sometimes it takes years. But, I emphasize again, God can use us at any point in our Christian walk—the secret is to stay focused on Him.

I'm sure many can relate to my struggles with patience. It wasn't until a few years after I had moved on from my time at the Christian retreat centre, where I lived and worked, that I saw God's sense of humour. The rooms there all have names relating to different spiritual virtues, such as Peace, Courage, Wisdom, etc.

The room that I had as my own was called *Patience!*

There are numerous examples throughout scripture of people who have had to wait for years before they saw a fulfillment of something God had planned for them. David was just a sixteen-year-old teenager when he was anointed by the prophet Samuel to be King of Israel, but it was many years (possibly thirty) before this became a reality. In the meantime, he went through a lot of trials and tests, through which his faith and trust in God grew stronger.

Moses was called to deliver Israel from Egyptian bondage and slavery, but had to wait forty years. Then he had to wait another forty years for the Promised Land, which he saw from a distance but never entered. And what about Jacob, who waited seven years for a wife and then was tricked by her father into working another seven years before he could marry her?

I'm not sure how patient I would have been. The point of this chapter has been to illustrate how we can be used by God at any point, really, as long as our hearts are open to Him. Our lives should be open books for anyone to read. Non-Christians study us all the time to see if we *walk* the *talk*. If we want to be ready to be used by God, we really do need to ensure that we are being *fertilized and watered* regularly—just like the golf course.

We should never stop growing spiritually while we are on this earth, and we mustn't lose confidence in His ability to use us, no matter what stage of growth we are at in our relationship with Him.

> *And I am certain that God, who began the good work within you, will continue his work until it is finally finished on the day when Christ Jesus returns. (Philippians 1:6, NLT)*

## PERSONAL NOTES

_____

_____

_____

_____

_____

_____

_____

_____

_____

_____

# 7. Maintenance, Upkeep and More!

*"Finally, be strong in the Lord, and in the strength of His might. Put on the full armour of God, that you may be able to stand firm against the schemes of the devil." (Ephesians 6:10–11, NASB)*

THE GOLF COURSE HAS BEEN created to serve people. Its whole purpose is to be a blessing for those who will walk all over it, wear the grass thin, and leave all kinds of marks and scars. Few people realize all that is involved with maintaining playable conditions. Not many understand the ongoing work required, let alone the tremendous effort to transform the land into what it is today.

Opening day does not mean the work is finished, but that it really is just beginning. If all work now ceased and the course was left to itself, it would soon grow wild again. Hidden seeds, and roots not completely removed, will spring up, and weeds from neighbouring fields will blow over and seed themselves. Clearly, daily maintenance is necessary to keep it playable, because there will always be improvements and upgrades required, as well as continual repairs from daily use. Besides all this, damage can occur because of animals, insects, disease, or even the weather.

I think you get the idea. There will be many times when it will seem like a battle to keep the course from being overtaken.

Obviously, one person cannot do all the work. Many are needed to work together as a team for the continuing upkeep and care of all the varied aspects of the golf course. It would be foolishness if the owner suddenly decided to take over total care and responsibility of the course on their own and ignore the advice and experience of the professionals. It isn't hard to imagine how quickly the fairways, greens, tee-decks, and overall condition of the course would decline in quality if proper caretaking was spurned.

I remember a little par-3 course I used to golf at occasionally, years ago. I hadn't been to it for at least two or three years when I went to a wedding reception held in its main building located at the front of the property, close to the road. It was an old barn that had been renovated for such functions, and the golf pro shop was on the lower level at the rear. I was quite shocked when I went downstairs to look out over the fairways, only to discover that they weren't there anymore. Everything had been allowed to grow wild, to the point it was impossible to recognize it as a golf course anymore.

All they did was stop maintaining it.

There are people who have a similar attitude when it comes to taking care of their lives. They may even have known God in their youth, but as they become older, and perhaps more *established*, they forget the One who has blessed them with all they have and are. God, in His mercy, offers more than one warning to those who seek security in material possessions.

*Beware lest you forget the Lord your God by not keeping His commandments and His ordinances and His statutes which I am commanding you today; lest when you have eaten and are satisfied, and have built good houses and lived in them, and when your herds and your flocks multiply, and your silver and your gold multiply, and all that you have multiplies, then your heart becomes proud, and you forget the Lord your God... (Deuteronomy 8:11–14a, NASB)*

That was originally a warning to the nation of Israel, but it is one we can all take to heart, no matter how much silver or gold we have. It's also one our nation needs to pay heed to. Canada and the United States have both strayed far from the godly foundation they were built on.

Just as the golf course has been designed and built with a specific purpose in mind, we have been created to worship and bless our heavenly Father and fellowship with Him. He has work for us to do, that we may be a blessing to others.

> For we are His workmanship, created in Christ Jesus for good works, which God prepared beforehand, that we should walk in them. (Ephesians 2:10, NASB)

It isn't something people like to hear, but we are called to lay down our lives, to open our hearts to others, and—like the golf course—we risk being trodden and scarred. When it comes to abuse and rejection, Jesus quite literally wrote the book on the subject.

> For even Christ didn't please Himself. As the Scriptures say, "Those who insult you are insulting me." (Romans 15:3, NLT)

> For consider Him who has endured such hostility by sinners against Himself, so that you may not grow weary and lose heart. (Hebrews 12:3, NASB)

God has called us to *love*. Until we truly experience His love for ourselves, we cannot love others the way we are meant to. Human love falls very far short of God's love. There are many people with charitable hearts who do all kinds of *good works,* but in the light of eternity, it's all worthless. It is possible to feed and clothe the poor, to care for orphans, etc., but not know God. Scripture describes the *righteous deeds* of man to be nothing more than *filthy rags*.

I recall the account of a godly man who was in India several years ago. He told how one day, as he was walking through the back streets of one city, he suddenly came upon the carcass of a cow that had died. These creatures are worshipped, so nobody was permitted to remove it. As he struggled with the gut-wrenching stink of such a large, rotting beast, he sensed the Lord saying to him that this overwhelming stench was how God reacts to our own self-righteousness.

That's a pretty gruesome illustration, but it does get the point across. We need to be filled with God's love. Religious rituals and rules won't do it. They only bring death and the stink of self-righteousness. There are people who have sincerely tried to help others but end up getting so wounded for their efforts that they're the ones who need help. So, in order to love the way God has called us to, we need to love Him first and be *filled* with His love.

*And you shall love the Lord you God with all your heart, and with all your soul, and with all your mind, and with all your strength. The second is this, "You shall love your neighbour as yourself." There is no other commandment greater than these. (Mark 12:30–31, NASB)*

*This is my commandment, that you love one another, just as I have loved you. Greater love has no one than this, that one lay down his life for his friends. (John 15:12–13, NASB)*

It would be awful if, after so much has been done to create such a fine new golf course, no one knew about it. That's why the owner will try to inform as many as possible. People now need to be notified of the new choice they have. Advertisements, flyers, maps, etc., need to be sent out and set up, all with clear directions so the public will not only know about the new course, but also how to get there.

I know of some golf courses that are extremely difficult to find. Directions to them are rather vague, unless you've already been there. Other places, in contrast, have people whose only job is to promote the golf course.

Our responsibility, as Christians, is to tell others the Good News of Jesus, and to show them the way to God. We need to be aware that our lives are *maps* which non-Christians are studying all the time. We should be conscious of how good a map we are.

*And He said to them, "Go into all the world and preach the gospel to all creation." (Mark 16:15, NASB)*

*Now all these things are from God, who reconciled us to Himself through Christ, and gave us the ministry of reconciliation, namely, that God was in Christ reconciling the world to Himself, not counting their trespasses against them, and He has committed to us the word of reconciliation. Therefore, we are ambassadors for Christ, as though God were entreating through us; we beg you on behalf of Christ, be reconciled to God. (2 Corinthians 5:18–20, NASB)*

God does not want people to die without knowing Him. More than that, He doesn't want people to waste their lives living without Him. I learned about God when I was a young boy, but I didn't actually receive Him as my Lord and Saviour until I was twenty-four years old. Everyone is different. Some live their whole lives and are on their deathbeds before they accept Jesus into their hearts, if at all. The point is, God is faithful and patient, more than we deserve.

*The Lord is not slow about His promise, as some count slowness, but is patient toward you, not*

> *wishing for any to perish but for all to come to*
> *repentance. (2 Peter 3:9, NASB)*

> *[Strive to] save others, snatching [them] out of*
> *[the] fire; on others take pity [but] with fear,*
> *loathing even the garment spotted by the flesh*
> *and polluted by their sensuality. (Jude 1:22–23,*
> *AMP)*

It should be becoming clear that God really does not want anyone to be lost. But for those who do not choose Him, there are eternal consequences. People without understanding always try to argue that if God loved us so much, why does He send people to hell? Hell is a very real place, by the way. People don't like to hear about it, and most pastors and ministers today shy away from preaching about it, which I think is a mistake.

The truth is, God does not send anyone to hell. *People send themselves to hell by rejecting God!* It is as tragically simple as that.

Understand this: God created hell for the devil and his fallen angels. Hell was never intended for people!

Out of love for God and all He has done for us, we must reach out to those around us who have not yet experienced the true love of God in their lives.

Like the golf course that has not been maintained and is overrun, there are Christians who have let the enemy overtake them by not allowing God to continue to *renew* or *maintain* them. The book of Acts reports how the early church met together often, and they were continually being *filled* and *renewed* by the Holy Spirit.

We need to watch that undetected roots and seeds planted by the enemy don't begin to grow again—and we all have some.

> *See to it that no one comes short of the grace of God; that no root of bitterness springing up causes trouble, and by it the many be defiled. (Hebrews 12:15, NASB)*

Just as it is impossible for one person to take care of a golf course alone, we need other Christians.

> *And let us not neglect our meeting together, as some people do, but encourage one another, especially now that the day of his return is drawing near. (Hebrews 10:25, NLT)*
> *Therefore, confess your sins to one another, and pray for one another, so that you may be healed. The effective prayer of a righteous man can accomplish much. (James 5:16, NASB)*

We do need others to help keep us on track. The man I confronted about his spiritual pride didn't like it, but we were able to pray together. Not only did he change, but I learned a lot, too. As much as we should be open to correction, we also need to affirm and encourage one another.

We are all different, and that's okay. Just as it takes many different people with different skills to look after a golf course, so too, God has called us to do different jobs. He has equipped each of us differently.

> *Now you are Christ's body, and individually members of it. And God has appointed in the church, first apostles, second prophets, third teachers, then miracles, then gifts of healings, helps, administrations, various kinds of tongues. (1 Corinthians 12:27–28, NASB)*

> *For just as we have many members in one body and all the members do not have the same function, so we, who are many, are one body in Christ, and individually members one of another. And since we have gifts that differ according to the grace given to us, let each exercise them accordingly: if prophecy, according to the proportion of his faith; if service, in his serving; or he who teaches, in his teaching; or he who exhorts, in his exhortation; he who gives, with liberality; he who leads, with diligence; he who shows mercy, with cheerfulness. (Romans 12:4–8, NASB)*

We *must* work together to *honour* and *accept* one another within the body of Christ. Now, this doesn't mean that we have to accept sinful behaviour. Not at all. That's what being accountable to one another is all about. Love covers a multitude of sins, and we must lovingly correct, reprove, and help each other. Nowhere does scripture give us licence to lord it over others as though we are better than them.

> *For through the grace given to me I say to every-*
> *one among you not to think more highly of himself*
> *than he ought to think... (Romans 12:3, NASB)*

People are guilty of both extremes. Either there is no room for mercy—only condemnation for sin—or there is acceptance of the sin as well as the person. Neither approach is scriptural.

There are main-line denominations today which have strayed away from God's Word. The whole homosexuality issue is a prime example. *We are to love all men and women—no matter what they do or how they choose to live.* That is what God wants us to do, but that does not mean we are to accept their sin or pretend it is acceptable, even if the laws of our land would say otherwise.

I recently met a man who was in a position of leadership within a local church—a main-line denomination in Canada. He has decided that he wants to be a woman and has taken steps to *change*.

This is wrong!

Even the most liberal-minded in society will initially feel or sense how wrong this is, if they are honest. But they will still go out of their way to accept such a decision, because they think this is how to accept and love the *person*.

Any parent knows that if their child is about to do something which will hurt them, they will step in and stop them. Unfortunately, the church leadership chose to ignore the clear Word of God and actually encouraged that man, and it isn't an isolated case. The governing bodies of most churches actually endorse policies that totally contradict the Word of God. The moral decline of society has permeated into and undermined the godly standards within the church.

When I first became a Christian, I met a person named Janet at the drop in centre I had discovered in the mall where I worked. Janet sincerely loved the Lord, and did a lot of volunteer work around the centre. About five years later, we all discovered that Janet was actually John. That was quite a shock, but the good news is that John really did love God and was growing and maturing as a Christian.

God was finally able to show John that he had been deceived and that it was time to put things right, as much as possible. There was, of course, mixed response to this news, but ultimately, those who knew him tried to convey the love and support that he needed at that critical time.

How much damage could have been done if we had either condemned and spurned John, or said to him, "It's okay to be like that—God loves you, don't you know?"

Leighton Ford is quoted as saying, "God loves us the way we are, but too much to leave us that way."

As we really begin to *know* Jesus, we also begin to know Truth. When the light of Truth grows stronger in our lives, satan's lies are revealed. My friend John discovered this as he grew in his relationship with Jesus. He was eventually able to see the truth about who he was, and was then able to recognize the lies of the enemy that he had believed. By getting to know Jesus, who said of Himself, *"I am the Way, the Truth, and the Life"* (John 14:6, NLT), John was set free—just as scripture declares.

*Then you will know the truth, and the truth will set you free. (John 8:32, NIV)*

To love others as God loves us is a high and holy calling. And we certainly can't do it alone or in our own strength. We need to learn to seek God and be filled with His love to the point that we *overflow*. As we all learn to do this throughout the nations, we will become the Church of Christ which God has meant for us to be.

*So then let us pursue the things which make for peace and the building up of one another. (Romans 14:19, NASB)*

> *Be on the alert, stand firm in the faith, act like men, be strong. Let all that you do be done in love. (1 Corinthians 16:13–14, NASB)*

I think I've made it clear that we need to be diligent to guard our hearts and continue to grow as Christians, because the enemy will continue to plant his seeds amongst us. For this reason, we cannot grow slack or careless. We need to recognize that there is a battle going on, and we're in it whether we like it or not. But we also have to have a clear perspective of who our enemy is. Hate the sin but love the sinner, to put it simply.

> *For we are not fighting against people made of flesh and blood, but against the evil rulers and authorities of the unseen world, against those mighty powers of darkness who rule this world, and against wicked spirits in the heavenly realms. (Ephesians 6:12, NLT)*

The Blood of Jesus, applied to every area of our lives, is more *powerful* than any fungicide or weed-killer. *Nothing can stand against the Blood!* It testifies throughout the *visible* and *invisible* realms that satan has been *defeated!*

When I was at the Christian retreat centre years ago, we encountered many interesting learning curves. As we learned to pray for and minister into peoples' lives, sometimes there would be demonic manifestations. This was new to many of us, and I believe God allowed us to experience what we did to teach us about the authority that we have *in Him*.

One time, we were praying for a lady who needed a lot of ministry. As the others were praying, a couple of us were singing in the background, because we had learned that it helped when we worshipped God during ministry. He does say that He inhabits the praises of His people.

When we began to sing the song, *There's Power in the Blood*, the woman started to cry out for us to stop. Actually, it was the demon speaking through her. As we continued to sing, it described what it saw in the spiritual realm to be a wave of blood coming and washing over it, one crimson wave after another, and each time it would moan in agony, "Oh no, here it comes again."

As serious and enlightening as this was, it was also humorous. We did finally make the thing shut up, and ordered it to leave, which it was forced to do because it couldn't stand the torment of being washed by the Blood of Jesus.

*And they overcame him [satan] because of the blood of the lamb and because of the word of their testimony, and they did not love their life even to death. (Revelation 12:11, NASB)*

In the world today, we don't have to look far to see the destruction caused by demonic seeds and their bad fruit flourishing everywhere. Just as God is sowing good seed, satan is busy sowing bad. And make no mistake—satan will use *whoever* he can to carry out his destructive plans.

> *And He answered and said, "The one who sows good seed is the Son of Man, and the field is the world; and as for the good seed, these are the sons of the kingdom; and the tares are the sons of the evil one; and the enemy who sowed them is the devil, and the harvest is the end of the age; and the reapers are angels." (Matthew 13:37–39, NASB)*

God has already determined the end. Again I repeat, the enemy *has been defeated* and *his end has been prepared!* The enemy thought he had won by getting Jesus to be crucified, but, by the power of God's Holy Spirit, Jesus rose from the dead. The legal obligation of death, which satan knew only too well and demanded, *was fulfilled*, and now *satan has no power* to hold onto or keep Jesus down.

> *Therefore just as the tares are gathered up and burned with fire, so shall it be at the end of the age. The Son of Man will send forth His angels, and they will gather out of His kingdom all stumbling blocks, and those who commit lawlessness, and will cast them into the furnace of fire; in that place there shall be weeping and gnashing of*

*teeth. Then the righteous will shine forth as the sun in the kingdom of their Father. He who has ears, let him hear. (Matthew 13:40–43, NASB)*

As Christians, we must not grow weary and discouraged or lose sight of whom or what we are doing battle with. If the devil was always watching Jesus to find a way to tempt him, how much more do we need to be alert to his tactics?

*For though we walk in the flesh, we do not war according to the flesh, for the weapons of our warfare are not of the flesh, but divinely powerful for the destruction of fortresses. We are destroying speculations and every lofty thing raised up against the knowledge of God, and we are taking every thought captive to the obedience of Christ..." (2 Corinthians 10:3–5, NASB)*

All this talk about spiritual warfare makes some Christians uncomfortable, but it is a reality that has been ongoing for a long time.

*And from the days of John the Baptist until now the kingdom of heaven suffers violence, and the violent men take it by force. (Matthew 11:12, NASB)*

107

If you read the story of Daniel, in the Old Testament, you'll see how the angels have to do battle. Chapter 10 clearly tells of the angel Gabriel who was forced to do battle for twenty-one days with the demonic *prince* of the kingdom of Persia. Only when the angel Michael came to help was Gabriel able to continue on to Daniel. When he had finished speaking with the man, he explained that he had to return to fight against the satanic angel of Persia, and he also warned that another demonic *prince* was coming.

There is much happening in the invisible realm today that would defy imagination if we could see. Consequently, we *must* maintain fellowship with God and His people. As long as we stay close to Him, we will find the strength and courage needed for whatever He has for us each day.

> *...and indeed our fellowship is with the Father, and with His Son Jesus Christ. (1 John 1:3, NASB)*

> *But the Lord is faithful, and He will strengthen and protect you from the evil one. (2 Thessalonians 3:3, NASB)*

Those are encouraging promises. An earlier scripture mentioned *bringing every thought captive to Christ*. It should be noted that *our mind is the battlefield* where the enemy works the hardest. That's a major reason why I have tried to emphasize the need to read God's Word *daily*.

When we become Christians, we are given the Holy Spirit, who will help us learn what we need to, but it's up to us to develop good habits. Circumstances often seem overwhelming, and it's easy to lose sight of who we are and the authority we have in Christ. We forget too easily that God has given us gifts to use and He wants to teach us how to use them.

> *And for this reason I remind you to kindle afresh the gift of God which is in you through the laying on of my hands. For God has not given us a spirit of timidity, but of power and love and discipline. (2 Timothy 1:6–7, NASB)*

The enemy knows that we will be unstoppable if we all join together and become *unified in Christ*. Why do you think there are so many denominations, so many religions, in the world today? God never intended it to be this way. But the relentless works of darkness continue to sow seeds of division whenever and wherever possible. Those who would stand against evil need to be prepared to pay the price. Jesus told us that if the world hated Him, it will hate us, too.

> *Therefore do not be ashamed of the testimony of our Lord, or of me His prisoner; but join with me in suffering for the gospel according to the power*

*of God, who has saved us and called us with a holy calling, not according to our works, but according to His own purpose and grace which was granted us in Christ Jesus from all eternity, but now has been revealed by the appearing of our Saviour Christ Jesus, who abolished death, and brought life and immortality to light through the gospel... (2 Timothy 1:8–10, NASB)*

*Therefore encourage one another, and build up one another, just as you also are doing. (1 Thessalonians 5:11, NASB)*

As the spiritual temperature increases in individual lives, families, and nations around the world, there is a need like never before to seek the face of God, to *know* Him— that we may be the people He has called us to be!

*So let us know, let us press on to know the Lord. His going forth is as certain as the dawn; and He will come to us like the rain, like the spring rain watering the earth. (Hosea 6:3, NASB)*

*Call to Me, and I will answer you, and I will tell you great and mighty things, which you do not know. (Jeremiah 33:3, NASB)*

I urge you today, *choose God!* The heat of His wrath will soon be released upon this earth, and all men *will* stand before Him to be judged.

If you know your heart is not right with Him, don't wait any longer. Time truly is running out. Don't put off making a decision for God another day. Cry out to Him—call upon His name!

> *And it shall be, that everyone who calls on the name of the Lord shall be saved. (Acts 2:21, NASB)*

> *For God says, "At just the right time, I heard you. On the day of salvation, I helped you." Indeed, the "right time" is now. Today is the day of salvation. (2 Corinthians 6:2, NLT)*

# PERSONAL NOTES

_____

_____

_____

_____

_____

_____

_____

_____

_____

_____

_____

_____

_____

_____

_____

_____

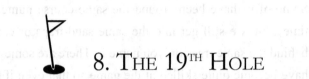

# 8. THE 19TH HOLE

*"Jesus answered and said to him, 'Truly, truly, I say to you, unless one is born again, he cannot see the kingdom of God.'"*

> *Nicodemus said to Him, 'How can a man be born when he is old? He cannot enter a second time into his mother's womb and be born, can he?'*

> *Jesus answered, 'Truly, truly, I say to you, unless one is born of water and the Spirit, he cannot enter the kingdom of God. That which is born of the flesh is flesh, and that which is born of the Spirit is spirit.*

> *"Do not marvel that I said to you, 'You must be born again.'*

*"The wind blows where it wishes and you hear the sound of it, but do not know where it comes from and where it is going; so is everyone who is born of the Spirit." (John 3:3–8, NASB)*

**I**N CONCLUSION, I'D LIKE TO shift the focus a bit, from the golf course to playing the game itself.

All of us are at various stages along the course, and we each vary considerably in our ability to play the game. Some of us have been around the same course numerous times, but we still get into the same sand-traps or caught behind the same trees or, you name it. There are some who have become quite skilled at the game so that even if they land in the rough, experience has taught them how to get out quickly without adding unnecessary penalty strokes.

Others are on their final round—*no one knows when that will be*—but no matter where we are, how poorly or how well we play, we all will eventually meet together at the clubhouse at the end of the game.

However, this clubhouse is extremely particular about who it lets in. Standards are so high, in fact, that *none of us qualify* on our own merit, no matter how well we may have scored in the final round!

> ...*and nothing unclean and no one who practices abomination and lying, shall ever come into it, but only those whose names are written in the Lamb's book of life. (Revelation 21:27, NASB)*

"But," you say, "I haven't done anything *abominable;* certainly nothing to deserve this. I'm not a liar."

Really?

*If we say that we have no sin, we are deceiving ourselves, and the truth is not in us. (1 John 1:8, NASB)*

Not convinced yet? It's easy to see that you're not as bad as those *other* people you see in the news who do horrible things. Let's look at the standard Jesus set for us. He said that even if we *think* wrongly we're guilty. For example, if we hate anyone, no matter how justified our feelings may be, it's still considered to be as wrong as murder.

"But, I'm a good person. I go to church…sometimes. At least, I believe in God."

An important point to make here is there's a huge difference between *believing* in God and *knowing God personally*. Let's look at some more scripture:

*And this is the message we have heard from Him and announce to you, that God is light, and in Him there is no darkness at all. If we say that we have fellowship with Him and yet walk in the darkness, we lie and do not practice the truth; but if we walk in the light as He Himself is in the light, we have fellowship with one another, and the blood of Jesus His Son cleanses us from all sin. If we say we have no sin, we are deceiving ourselves, and the truth is not in us. If we confess our sins, He is faithful and righteous to forgive us*

*our sins and to cleanse us from all unrighteous-*
*ness. If we say that we have not sinned, we make*
*Him a liar, and His word is not in us. (1 John*
*1:5–10, NASB)*

For those who have ears to hear, those are good words. All we have to do is confess to God that we have sinned and ask Him to forgive us, and He assures us that He hears us and He will forgive and cleanse us. This is what Jesus has done for us.

God is the owner of the clubhouse—to continue with our illustration. He has made provision for us to enter. He really wants everyone to know Him personally and come and enjoy all that He has prepared for them.

That's why He sent His Son out into the golf course to team up with all who would invite Him to be their partner. With the Owner's Son as our partner, we have a guaranteed pass to the clubhouse, and we are able to enjoy all the privileges of being a member as we play!

Think of it—He designed and built the course, and He wrote the rulebook. Who better to have as our partner?

And yet some still choose to arrogantly do it their own way, making up their own rules as they go. The enemy also gets mixed up in the game by handing out other rulebooks. Just look at all the religious cults in the world today and all of their faithful followers. How many times have you heard it said, "All roads lead to God?" Unfortunately, once they reach the clubhouse and discover they can't get in, it will be too late. The result will be much worse than simply being locked out of a building.

Notice the subtlety of the lie that the enemy has propagated. All of us will indeed go to heaven—we all will stand before God on the great and terrible day of Judgment! And it will be a terrible day for those who didn't choose the Son to be their partner, because their name will not be on the guest list. Those are the ones who will be turned away, locked out and sent to hell for eternity.

But the enemy was right—they got to go to heaven—briefly.

*And if anyone's name was not found written in the book of life, he was thrown into the lake of fire. (Revelation 20:15, NASB)*

I'm not making this up. This is God's Word. What so few realize is that it is the Owner's abundant graciousness all along by which anyone is even allowed to be on the course. Indeed, if the Son hadn't come to us, not only would we not have a way into the clubhouse, we wouldn't be playing at all!

The day is coming, known only to the Owner, when He will close down the golf course and, I repeat, all who are playing who haven't asked His Son to be their partner will have to stand before Him in judgment. When the Son is our partner, our names are written down in the Book of Life. Think of it as the membership book for the clubhouse.

*Heaven and earth will pass away, but My words will not pass away. But of that day or hour no one knows, not even the angels in heaven, nor the Son, but the Father alone. Take heed, keep on the alert; for you do not know when the appointed time is. (Mark 13:31–33, NASB)*

These are the Words of Jesus. He is telling his disciples, and us, that there is going to be judgment upon all the earth. He clearly describes events to watch for so that we will be ready.

*And there will be signs in the sun and moon and stars, and upon the earth dismay among nations, in perplexity at the roaring of the sea and the waves, men fainting from fear and the expectation of the things which are coming upon the world; for the powers of the heavens will be shaken.*

*And then they will see THE SON OF MAN COMING IN A CLOUD with power and great glory. But when these things begin to take place, straighten up and lift your heads, because your redemption is drawing near. (Luke 21:25–28, NASB)*

We can see evidence of this shaking in the world today. Never before in the history of this earth have there been so many successive catastrophes—earthquakes, tsu-namis, hurricanes, tornadoes, etc.

We need to be careful not to become numb to the news headlines, but realize *we are living in days that Jesus told us to be ready for.*

*Be on guard, that your hearts may not be weighed down with dissipation and drunkenness and the worries of life, and that day come on you sud-denly like a trap; for it will come upon all those who dwell on the face of the earth. But keep on the alert at all times, praying in order that you may have strength to escape all these things that are about to take place, and to stand before the Son of Man. (Luke 21:34–36, NASB)*

Those are certainly sobering words, but we should also be encouraged. As we rapidly approach the days of tribula-tion, if we have Jesus in our heart as our *partner* and as we keep our eyes on Him every day, we don't need to worry about anything or be surprised or unprepared concerning what is going on in the world.

*But take heed; behold, I have told you everything in advance. (Mark 13:23, NASB)*

Therefore, let's make sure we have Jesus as our partner as we play the course. He not only ensures entrance to the clubhouse at the end of the game—and deliverance from terrible judgment soon to come—but it's amazing all that He can teach us about improving our swing and reducing the number of strokes we take. We can't help but become better players with Him by our side. He will even be with us when we get into the thickest rough and show us how to get out.

*All we have to do is ask!*

It doesn't matter where you're at in the game—if you've just started or if you're on the final round; it doesn't matter how terribly you've played, or how well; He will come and join up with anyone at any point.

*He is ready and waiting for the invitation!*


*For God so loved the world, that He gave*
*His only begotten Son, that whoever believes in*
*Him should not perish, but have eternal life.*
 *(John 3:16, NASB)*

# PERSONAL NOTES

_____

_____

_____

_____

_____

_____

_____

_____

_____

_____

_____

_____

_____

_____

_____

_____

_____

# ABOUT THE AUTHOR

Craig Duncan Wood was born in 1956 (in Toronto, ON), and was baptized as a baby in the Presbyterian Church. As a child he grew up attending Sunday school at the United Church of Canada. At the age of 16 he decided that God didn't exist, so he turned away from anything to do with church.

Eight years later, at the age of 24, he began watching a weekly Christian program on television, called the 700 Club, and eventually prayed with the host to accept Jesus Christ as his savior. He has been a born-again, Spirit filled Christian since 1980.

Craig has always enjoyed expressing his creative talents whenever possible. Painting, photography (he is a graduate of Sheridan College of Applied Arts and Technology), playing guitar and song writing (he has been a worship leader for over 25 years), and even landscaping and gardening, have been his most common outlets.

He has always had a love for creative writing. This book, and his 'Jasharian Chronicles' novels, are his newest personal and creative endeavors.

Craig and his wife currently live in Shelburne, ON.